Rome and Byzantium

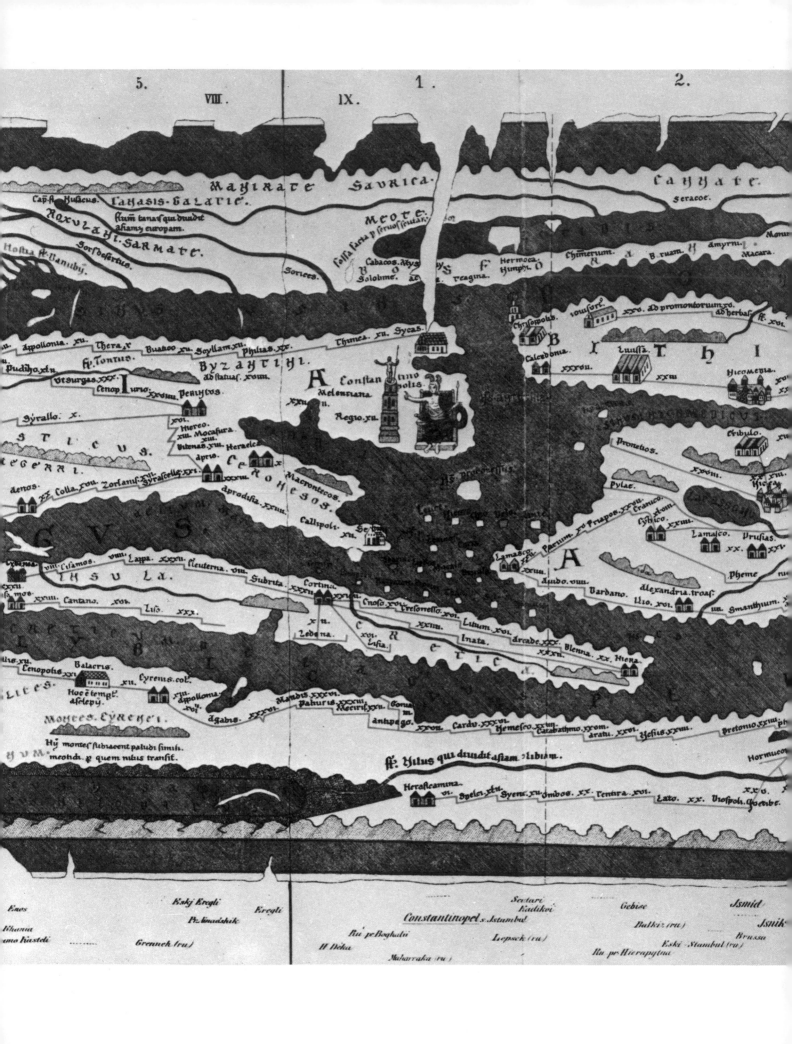

The Making of the Past

Rome and Byzantium

*by Clive Foss
and Paul Magdalino*

ELSEVIER · PHAIDON

Advisory Board for
The Making of the Past

John Boardman
Reader in Classical Archaeology, University of Oxford

Basil Gray
Former Keeper of Oriental Antiquities, British Museum

David Oates
Professor of Western Asiatic Archaeology,
Institute of Archaeology, University of London

Courtlandt Canby
Initiating Editor of the Series

Series Editor Graham Speake
Managing Editor Giles Lewis
Picture Editors Hilary Kay, Andrew Lawson
Design Richard Brookes
Visual Aids Roger Gorringe, Errol Bryant, Dick Barnard
Production Elizabeth Digby Firth

Frontispiece: All roads lead to Constantinople. Constantinople, the Sea of Marmora and the adjacent coasts in the Peutinger Table, originally drawn in the 4th century to show the road system which the government was always careful to maintain. After the original in the Imperial Library, Vienna.

ISBN 0 7290 0012 5

Elsevier-Phaidon, an imprint of Phaidon Press Ltd,
Littlegate House, St Ebbe's Street, Oxford

Planned and produced by Elsevier International Projects Ltd, Oxford, © 1977 Elsevier Publishing Projects SA, Lausanne. All rights reserved. No part of this publication may be reproduced, stored in a retrieval system, or transmitted, in any form or by any means, electronic, mechanical, photocopying, recording or otherwise, without the prior permission of the Publishers.

Origination by Art Color Offset, Rome, Italy

Filmset by Keyspools Limited, Golborne, Lancs.

Printed and bound by Brepols, Turnhout, Belgium

Contents

Maps

Preface to the series

This book is a volume in the Making of the Past, a series describing
the early history of the world as revealed by archaeology and related
disciplines. The series is written by experts under the guidance of a
distinguished panel of advisers and is designed for the layman, for
young people, the student, the armchair traveler and the tourist. Its
subject is a new history – the making of a new past, uncovered and
reconstructed in recent years by skilled specialists. Since many of the
authors of these volumes are themselves practicing archaeologists,
leaders in a rapidly changing field, the series is completely
authoritative and up-to-date. Each volume covers a specific period
and region of the world and combines a detailed survey of the modern
archaeology and sites of the area with an account of the early
explorers, travelers, and archaeologists concerned with it. Later
chapters of each book are devoted to a reconstruction in text and
pictures of the newly revealed cultures and civilizations that make up
the new history of the area.

Introduction

For over 1,000 years the city of Constantinople was one of the wonders of the world, with its port full of merchants from every corner of the earth, its magnificent buildings and its overpowering riches. The city was the capital of an equally fabulous empire – for most of the Middle Ages the largest, richest and most organized state in Europe – with the prestige due to the heir of the Romans and with vast resources accruing from regular taxation and extensive trade. When the city was founded by Constantine the Great in 330 AD, its domains encompassed the entire Mediterranean world and western Europe; when it fell to the Turks 1,100 years later, its power was virtually bounded by its walls. We shall trace this long and moving history, examining not only the events and the people, but also the characteristic monuments of the civilization. We shall begin in the early 3rd century AD with the empire vast and flourishing, and follow its fortunes down to the fall of Constantinople in 1453. Our focus will always be on the lands under imperial control, so that the geographical area discussed becomes smaller and smaller; but the independent civilizations which grew on the ruins of Rome are outside the scope of this book.

The period we shall consider falls into two unequal divisions – late antiquity, from the 3rd century to the 7th, and the Byzantine age which ends with the fall of Constantinople. The first period is the continuation of the Roman Empire – a world state based on an urban civilization, with common Classical institutions and culture which admitted a rich and colorful local variety. It was an age which showed its prosperity and power in the construction of a great range of monumental buildings, public and private. The Byzantine period saw fundamental changes as the state adapted to the new realities of barbarian invasions and curtailed dominions. Society took on new forms, clearly reflected in the castles, churches and palaces which remained predominant until the end.

In the introductory chapter we consider how the eastern empire came to the attention of the modern Europeans, tracing the process back to the antiquarian travelers of the Renaissance. Scholarly interest in the Byzantines, active since the 17th century, reached a climax in the work of Edward Gibbon, whose eloquent disdain for the period made a profound impression. In the 19th century historians of Christian art and architecture discovered a new world in Asia Minor and the eastern provinces, at the same time as the new science of archaeology was beginning to illustrate the transition from the ancient to the Byzantine world.

This long tradition of research has produced a remarkable picture of the periods, a picture which we examine in Chapters 2, 3 and 4. We first present the history of late antiquity, beginning at the death of Septimius Severus in 211 AD, when the empire was at its height, proceeding through the disasters of the 3rd century to the fundamental reforms of Diocletian and Constantine, which produced an absolutist, Christian state with its headquarters in the Greek-speaking east. The period saw the collapse of Roman rule in the west – erroneously called "the fall of the Roman Empire" – and the ambitious attempt of Justinian to recover the lost provinces. We include a sketch of social and economic conditions, but shall have little to say of literature or ecclesiastical history. A survey of the monuments of late antiquity will illustrate the variety of life in the empire, from the thatched roofs of Britain to the desert monasteries of Egypt, and show at the same time the remarkable uniformity of culture.

The Byzantine age follows in Chapter 4, with its triumphs over the Arabs and Slavs, and the internal danger of the iconoclastic controversy. The triumphs led to the glorious days of the Macedonian dynasty, when Byzantine arms again approached Rome and the Holy Land, only to yield to a precipitate collapse before the Turks, a partial recovery under the Komnenoi, then the disaster of the Fourth Crusade which temporarily created a Latin empire in place of the Byzantine. Although Constantinople was recaptured, the Byzantines never regained their strength, and the state slowly disintegrated.

The Byzantine state was dominated by religion. Chapter 5 will consider the vital role of the Orthodox Church – its origins and differences from Latin Christianity, its relations with the state, its place in the life of the population, its liturgy and the importance of its monks and monasteries. Because almost all surviving Byzantine art is religious, icons and iconography and the relationship of art to religion will also be presented. We conclude by asking what the Byzantine civilization accomplished and what value it has for the modern world, identifying the various cultural streams which formed the society, and illustrating the survival of the Byzantine ideal.

Chronological Table

	EMPERORS		EVENTS
	(Emperors not mentioned in the text are omitted.)		
AD 193–211	Septimius Severus		
211–17	Caracalla		
222–35	Severus Alexander	227	Foundation of the Sasanian dynasty in Persia
235–38	Maximinus		
244–49	Philip "the Arab"		
249–51	Decius	251	Roman army destroyed by the Goths
253–60	Valerian		
259–68	Postumus (in Gaul)	260	Valerian captured by the Persians
260–68	Gallienus		
267–72	Zenobia	259–73	"Gallic empire"
268–70	Claudius Gothicus		
270–75	Aurelian		
276–82	Probus		
282–83	Carus		
283–84	Numerian		
284–305	Diocletian		
287–93	Carausius (in Britain)		
286–305	Maximian		
293–306	Constantius I		
293–311	Galerius	303–13	The Great Persecution
306–12	Maxentius	312	Battle of the Milvian Bridge; "conversion" of Constantine
306–37	Constantine the Great		
		325	Council of Nicaea
		330	Foundation of Constantinople
337–61	Constantius II		
361–63	Julian "the Apostate"		
364–75	Valentinian I		
364–78	Valens		
367–83	Gratian		
379–95	Theodosius	378	Battle of Adrianople
383–88	Magnus Maximus (in Britain)		

IN THE WEST

	EMPERORS		EVENTS
395–423	Honorius	406	Germanic invasion of Gaul
407–11	Constantine III (in Britain)	410	Rome captured by Alaric
421	Constantius III	429–31	Vandal conquest of Africa
425–55	Valentinian III	430	Death of St Augustine
475–76	Romulus Augustulus, last western emperor	445–53	Invasions of Attila the Hun
		455	Rome sacked by the Vandals

IN THE EAST

	EMPERORS		EVENTS
395–408	Arcadius		
408–50	Theodosius II		
474–91	Zeno		
491–518	Anastasius		
527–65	Justinian	529	Codification of Roman law
		532–37	Construction of St Sophia
		533–54	Reconquest of Africa, Sicily and Italy
		542	The great plague
		568	Italy invaded by the Lombards

	EMPERORS		EVENTS
582–602	Maurice	589–628	Chosroes II emperor of Persia
602–10	Phokas	602–28	Great war between Rome and Persia; Greece and the Balkans invaded by Avars and Slavs
610–41	Heraclius		
641–68	Constans II	634–42	Arab conquest of Syria, Palestine and Egypt
668–85	Constantine IV	673–78	First Arab attack on Constantinople
685–95; 705–11	Justinian II	698	Carthage falls to the Arabs
717–41	Leo III	717–18	Arab siege of Constantinople
		726	Iconoclastic controversy begins
741–75	Constantine V	751	Ravenna falls to the Lombards
775–80	Leo IV	753	Iconoclastic council
780–97	Constantine VI	800	Coronation of Charlemagne
797–802	Irene		
802–11	Nikephoros	811	Byzantine army crushed by the Bulgars
813–20	Leo V		Second iconoclastic period begins
820–29	Michael of Armorion	822–24	Revolt of Thomas the Slav
829–42	Theophilos	826	Crete falls to the Arabs
842–67	Michael III	827–78	Sicily falls to the Arabs
		843	Restoration of the icons
		858–67; 877–86	Patriarchate of Photius
		860	First Russian attack on Constantinople
867–86	Basil I	863	Victory over the Arabs; Byzantine offensive in the east begins
886–912	Leo VI		
913–59	Constantine VII Porphyrogenitos	875–902	Byzantine reconquests in Italy and Sicily
919–44	Romanos Lekapenos		
963–69	Nikephoros Phokas		
969–76	John Tzimiskes	961	Reconquest of Crete
963–1025	Basil II	996–1018	Reconquest of Bulgaria
1042–54	Constantine IX Monomachos	1071	Battle of Manzikert; Bari falls to the Normans
1067–71	Romanos IV	1096	First Crusade
1081–1118	Alexios I		
1118–43	John II	1204	Fourth Crusade; capture of Constantinople
1143–80	Manuel I		
1182–85	Andronikos I	1204–61	Latin empire of Constantinople; empire of Nicaea
1185–95	Isaac II Angelos		
1195–1203	Alexios III		
1204–22	Theodore Laskaris	1204–1340	Despotate of Epirus
1222–54	John III Vatatzes	1204–1461	Empire of Trebizond
1258–82	Michael VIII Palaiologos	1261	Recapture of Constantinople
1282–1328	Andronikos II		
1328–41	Andronikos III	1288–1326	Osman, founder of the Ottoman dynasty
1341–91	John V		
1347–54	John VI Kantakouzenos	1354	Turks cross into Europe
1391–1425	Manuel I	1362–89	Murad I, Turkish sultan
1425–48	John VIII	1389–1402	Bayezid I, Turkish sultan
1449–53	Constantine XI	1402	Campaign of Tamerlane in Asia Minor
		1421–51	Murad II, sultan
		1451–81	Mehmet II, sultan
		1453	Fall of Constantinople
		1460	Fall of Mistra
		1461	Fall of Trebizond

1. The Discovery of Byzantium

The gateway to St John's Basilica, Ephesus. An engraving from E. G. Meyer's *A Town in the Balkans* (1809).

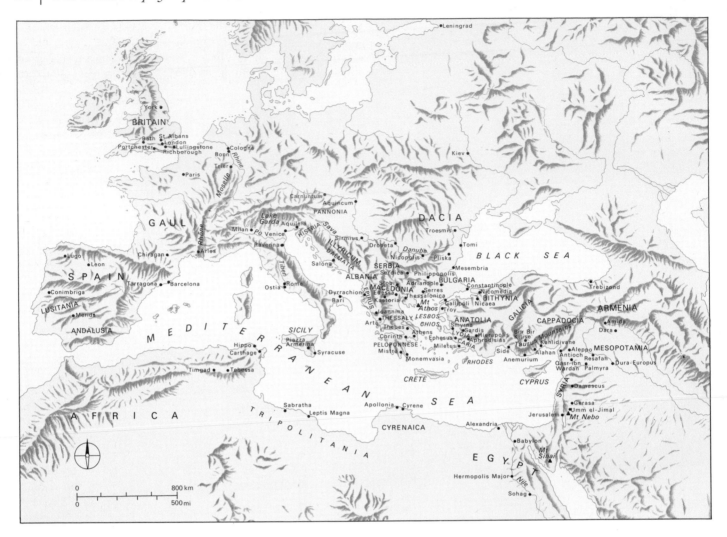

The Renaissance: travelers and antiquarians. The Italian Renaissance of the 14th and 15th centuries, which led to the European Renaissance of the 16th and 17th centuries, was characterized by its antiquarian obsession with the Greco-Roman world. This was hardly sufficient in itself to stimulate an interest in the Byzantine Empire, a society which survived until the mid-15th century and thus, as far as most Renaissance men were concerned, belonged to recent history. But it created a demand for the things which Byzantium had preserved from antiquity. Educated Byzantines were welcomed at European courts as teachers of Greek, and in the first flush of enthusiasm for things Hellenic, Byzantine texts were sought along with Classical ones. At the same time, western travelers to Greek lands became more aware of the need to pay attention to the material remains of past civilizations; the pioneer in this respect was Ciriaco d'Ancona, a merchant who on his business trips to the Aegean in the early 15th century amused himself by recording inscriptions, and collecting manuscripts and coins. By the 17th century, hardly any traveler to the Levant failed to seek out ancient ruins and to take away with him as many souvenirs as he could carry. Most were fairly indiscriminate about the objects they looted. While the fashion was for Classical statuary, the English ambassador to the sultan's court at Constantinople at the beginning of the 17th century, Sir Thomas Roe, was not above trying to remove the Golden Gate, the ceremonial marble portal by which the Byzantine emperors had entered the city. Even two centuries later, in the age of Lord Elgin, a British naval lieutenant, Adolphus Slade, dreamed of removing from Thessalonica "the pulpit whence St. Paul preached to the Thessalonians . . . It is formed of one block of marble, of a species of verd antique, and consists of three steps, with a platform the parapet of which reaches to the knee . . . It would be seen to much more advantage in London; and I dare say that the Sultan would give it to an ambassador if asked. A trifling gift afterwards to the pasha, and the Greek bishop of Salonica, would cause it to be embarked without opposition from the people."

As far as knowledge of Byzantium was concerned, the most important objects removed from the Levant were manuscripts. Again, the most coveted works were those of ancient authors, but these might be bound with Byzantine commentaries and imitative writings, and Byzantine works on law, theology and medicine were valued for

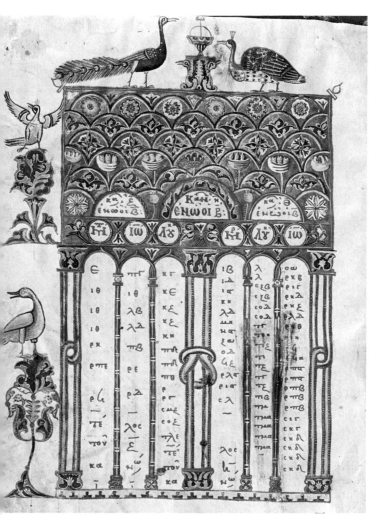

Above: canon tables from Mount Athos. Codex Dionysiou 356, dated 1585.

Opposite: the world of late antiquity.

Stavroniketa on Mount Athos, "It was a quarto of the tenth or eleventh century, and a most unexceptionable tome, which these unkind monks preferred keeping to themselves instead of letting me have it, as they ought to have done."

Almost every literate traveler to the Levant in the 16th and 17th centuries left an account of his journey. Very few of these works are now of major significance for the ancient or medieval historian. Travel within the Ottoman Empire was dangerous and restricted, and foreigners kept to well-beaten tracks, mainly those leading to Constantinople. Thus there are many descriptions of Corfu, Zakynthos, Crete, Rhodes, Chios, Smyrna, Gallipoli, Heraclea, Philippopolis and Adrianople; rather fewer of Thessalonica, Athens and the Aegean hinterland of Asia Minor; and almost none of the Greek and Anatolian interiors. Everything was an object of curiosity, and in writing their diaries and memoirs, the travelers observed no criteria of selection and analysis other than those imposed by their native intelligence. In Constantinople they were suitably impressed by the major and obvious monuments of the Christian period – Hagia Sophia, the triumphal columns, the "Palace of Constantine" (Tekfur Saray), the walls and the cisterns – but they showed little interest in the many minor Byzantine churches; de Monconys, who described the Pantokrator monastery and the fresco and mosaic decoration to be seen in the former refectory of the Peribleptos monastery, was a notable exception. Still, the voluminous literature of these Renaissance gentlemen is an improvement on the silence observed by their medieval precursors, the Venetian and Genoese merchants. The genre of the travelogue, which they created by their passion for observing and recording, continued until the middle of the 19th century to be the principal medium for the publication of archaeological knowledge.

Religion: the Reformation and Counter-Reformation. Throughout the Middle Ages, religion had provided one of the main motives for travel to the eastern Mediterranean. The Holy Places of Palestine were the ultimate goals of every Christian pilgrim, and in visiting them the western European came into contact with many reminders of Byzantium. Not only did the voyage there lead by way of Greek islands – notably Crete and Cyprus – but nearly all the sacred sites were administered by Greek monks. Single-minded pilgrims were rare after the 15th century, but the western Christian, whether Catholic or Protestant, was deeply affected by the Biblical or Patristic associations of the places he visited. The European traders maintained large depots at Smyrna, and one of the standard excursions to be made from there was a tour of the Seven Churches of the Apocalypse; on these tours, travelers paid special attention to the Christian antiquities still visible. The Byzantine churches at Nicaea (Iznik) and Chalcedon (Kadiköy) came in for special

their information. Since most manuscripts were procured for royal and princely libraries, prestige books were much in demand: codices that were richly illuminated, beautifully written or obviously of early date. The biggest collector was the French monarchy, which enjoyed favored status at the Ottoman court from the mid-16th century; French agents managed to remove 600 codices from the Seraglio, in which Mehmet II, conqueror of Constantinople, had deposited many books formerly belonging to the imperial library. In less spectacular ways, other travelers, working both for European governments and on their own account, procured manuscripts from monasteries all over the Greek world. The tradition continued until the end of the 19th century, when both the monasteries and their governments became convinced of the need for putting a stop to it. Almost the last, possibly the most honorable, and certainly the most engaging manuscript-hunter was the Englishman Robert Curzon. He remarked of a book which he found in the library of

The Antiphonitis church, dedicated to the Blessed Virgin, dating from the 12th century, near Hagios Amvrosios, northern Cyprus.

comment because of the ecumenical councils held in these places, while Ephesus, Thessalonica and Athens were memorable for the missionary activity of St Paul.

Western hostility to the Greek Orthodox Church ran deep, but the religious conflicts which divided Protestants and Catholics made westerners look to the Orthodox for moral support. Ultimately, neither side found what it was looking for, but in the process Byzantine religious institutions and patterns of worship came in for a lot of scrutiny. The Protestants early took an interest, partly because the Orthodox Church was opposed to Rome, and partly because the Greek liturgy and New Testament were obviously the closest linguistically to those of the early Church. It was a pupil of Philip Melancthon, Luther's humanist colleague, who produced the first printed editions of Byzantine chroniclers. Even Protestant invective could be informative. We owe the following account by Dr John Covel, English chaplain in Constantinople in the later 17th century, to the author's disgust at the many "popish" elements of Greek worship:

"[At Heraclea in Thrace] there are yet standing, in all, 40 Greek churches, yet (as elsewhere) none deserve the name but the Metropole's, which is a good old odde fashioned building. It hath a Cupola and half cupolas about it like Sta. Sophia.

"They show there, within the Metropolis, the top stone of Sta. Gluceria's tomb, which they say was saved out of her monastery, which stood hard by, but was ruin'd and most part tumbled into the Sea. It is pure white marble, about a foot thick, most neatly covered and hollowed on the edges, with a coronite around the head, and at the feet with two spires. At the head there is cut an archt hole, in which they say her head was kept; and there is a hole sideways of it which is like a saucer, and in the bottom of it is another small one, out of which they say continually issued an holy oyle. All this arch't hole was cover'd with a plate of gold; the pins that fasten'd it yet remain. I assure you the whole thing is absolutely the curiosest piece of work that is to be found in Greece of so modern artifice. On the upper side, between the arch't hole and the bottome, rose an inscription in impure Iambick. It was wrote in a moderne character, which is very difficult to be read, and the latter end of each verse was wrote under the former part in very much smaller letters. I verily believe this whole thing was but a piece of Greekish monkery, and they might have some pretty contrivance to let oyl, or the like liquor, drop upon occasion, to work some miracle upon the credulous."

The Roman Catholics felt equally disappointed in the Greek Church, which, perversely it seemed, would submit to any degree of humiliation at the hands of the sultan rather than listen to Catholic missionaries or accept the tutelage of a Catholic monarch. Yet Catholics and Orthodox undeniably had more in common than Orthodox and Protestants, and in trying to find a sound basis for her claim to be the Universal Church, Rome came closer to an intellectual, if not a spiritual understanding of the Byzantine religious legacy. The Roman establishment devoted large intellectual resources to justifying the traditions which the Reformation had called in question. In the process of justification, scholarly access to these traditions was greatly facilitated, as systematic attempts were made to publish basic materials, such as conciliar acts, saints' lives and liturgical texts, in a collected and critical way. Much of the Byzantine material included in fact represented a heritage common to both the eastern and the western churches, but the Byzantine Church of the period of schism also came in for a good deal of attention. Of particular significance was the work of two 16th-century Greek converts, Alemannus and Allatius.

The "Ancien Régime". The Catholic scholars who developed Byzantine studies in the 17th century – whether Jesuits, Dominicans, Benedictines or laymen – were all French. This was no accident. After the establishment of Catholicism as the official religion of France (1598), and with the progressive decline of Spain, the French monarchy naturally assumed the role of political champion of the papacy. The two great French regents of the first half of the century were both cardinals, and Louis XIV (1648–1715) included the eradication of Protestantism among his grand designs. But there was another factor which made the "grand siècle" of France a significant period in the development of Byzantine studies. This was the fundamental connection between Renaissance humanism and the cult of monarchy. Despite the "progressive" elements in the Renaissance – the emergence of the individual and the passion for secular knowledge – art and scholarship were dependent on the patronage of kings and princes. Monarchs used Classical philologists to glorify their image by means of the written word, in much the same way that they employed painters and musicians. This cast the humanist in a role similar to that of the Byzantine court rhetorician, and it made for a literate public which was not altogether unreceptive to Byzantine literature. There was much that a Renaissance monarch could learn from the Byzantine imperial cult, and, to judge from the huge number of manuscripts of the late Byzantine treatise on court ceremonial, the *De Officiis*, copied in Europe during the 16th and 17th centuries, this work may have been quite influential in creating the royal pageantry and mystique which culminated in Louis XIV's Versailles. Whatever the direct ideological antecedents of the French "Ancien Régime," this was, in its heyday of the 17th century, a society where Byzantium was likely to be considered a respectable subject for antiquarian research.

It was in the France of Louis XIV that the earliest, and possibly the greatest, Byzantinist of all time lived and wrote: Charles du Fresne du Cange (1610–88). Du Cange left a history of the Latin Empire of Constantinople, a study of Late Roman and Byzantine imperial families, a long essay on the topography of Constantinople, and Glossaries of medieval Latin and Greek. Du Cange's conclusions were as correct as they could have been with the material available to scholars at the time. His books, particularly the Glossaries, are still basic reference works, and his approach to prosopography (relating personalities to events) and topography has been followed by modern writers. Hardly less impressive than the man himself is the intellectual milieu which fashioned him, and put the tools and materials of research at his disposal. For the topography of Constantinople, he was particularly indebted to a book published a century before his time by Pierre Gilles (Gyllius), a zoologist whom Francis I had sent to the court of Suleiman the Magnificent, and who had made a very thorough attempt to reconstruct the layout of the Roman and Byzantine city.

The Enlightenment. By his use of the term "Byzantine," and by compiling a dictionary of "debased" Greek, du Cange made it clear that the society he was studying was neither purely Greek nor purely Roman. Yet neither he nor any contemporary tried to define what made Byzantine civilization distinctive, or when the break with antiquity occurred. Westerners of the 16th and 17th

Charles du Fresne du Cange (1610–88), possibly the greatest Byzantinist of all time.

centuries inherited from the Middle Ages the idea that Byzantium had forfeited the right to be considered the legitimate Roman Christian Empire because of the ecclesiastical schism, and had declined and fallen as a result of its sins: as one Elizabethan traveler put it, Constantinople "suffered divers fortunes under the Greekish empirors many years, insomutch that throughe their disgraces it went by little and little declineing." On the other hand, it could not be denied that the "Greeks" had ruled in unbroken succession from Constantine and Justinian, emperors whom the west had always been proud to claim as its own. The medieval argument that the Roman pope had the right to assume the authority forfeited by the emperor became less and less persuasive from the 15th century, when the *Donation of Constantine* (the document by which Constantine was supposed to have signed away his sovereignty to Pope Sylvester I) was exposed as a forgery, and Protestants naturally rejected any papal claim out of hand.

It was also a fact that Byzantium had preserved the learning which made Renaissance humanism possible. Inevitably, therefore, ideas about the decline of Rome and the status of Byzantium were subject to some confusion.

Westerners were fairly inconsistent in their opinions about the Byzantine cultural achievement. Where they thought of it as something recent, their taste was offended; thus Aubry de la Mottraye on the subject of Mt Athos, which he visited in 1699: "The Churches which are attached to these monasteries surpass all others of the Greeks in their construction and by their painted decoration, their images being the work of Muscovites or of Greeks from abroad, *who have derived from civilized Europe some taste and understanding of this fine art.*" But if Byzantium could be thought of as a lost civilization, it became respectable. George Sandys wrote in 1615 that Hagia Sophia "exceedeth . . . all other Fabricks whatsoever throughout the entire universe . . . The Roof compact and adorned with *Mosaick* painting. An antique kind of work, composed of little square pieces of Marble; guilded and coloured according to the place that they are to assume in the figure or ground: which set together, as if imbossed, present an unexpressible stateliness, and are of a marvellous durance . . . the Images (of admirable Workmanship and infinite in number) . . ." Like all travelers from the west, Sandys found the level of learning among the Greeks to be low, but he attributed it to the Ottoman domination: "A Nation once so excellent, that their precepts and examples do still remain as approved Canons to direct the mind that endeavoureth virtue . . . But now their knowledge is converted, as I may say, into affected ignorance (for they have no schools of learning amongst them), their liberty into contented slavery, *having lost their minds with their empire.*"

Pace hard-bitten Protestants like Dr Covel, the intellectual climate of the 17th century was still such as to give the Byzantines the benefit of the doubt. The following discussion of a popular tradition at Thebes by Jacob Spon well illustrates the mixture of skepticism and respect with which contemporaries viewed surviving Byzantine habits of thought: "a marble sepulchre, which they say is of St. Luke, in a church dedicated to him. But we read on it a Pagan epitaph of a certain *Nedymus*, in fine verses, which say nothing at all about St. Luke. The local priest told us that a lord of that district had put the body of St. Luke in that coffin, but in order not to expose it to the indiscreet zeal of the enemies of Christianity, he had added the epitaph of one of his own sons. This did not quite satisfy us. It occurred to me, so as not to object entirely to their tradition, that this could be the same St. Luke the Hermit of whom I have spoken, who might have been buried at first in the tomb of this Pagan which had been found empty, and that perhaps when the Convent of St. Luke had been built, they transported him there."

Clearly, European intellectuals needed a new perspective in which to view the decline of the Roman Empire: one which could reconcile their sense of achievement and optimism with the Renaissance concept of a

Opposite: the monastery of Dionysiou on Mount Athos. The foundation dates from the mid-14th century.

Edward Gibbon (1737–94), historian of the *Decline and Fall of the Roman Empire.*

decline from a golden age of Classical antiquity, and show how this decline underlay not only the "barbarism" of the west, but also the continuity of empire in the east. This perspective was supplied in the 18th-century intellectual movement known as the Enlightenment, which was essentially a French reaction against the obscurantism, traditionalism and authoritarianism of the Ancien Régime; this, it was held, was keeping men in the chains of the "Middle Ages" (a concept now formed for the first time), although the progress of science and representative government offered ways to freedom. Byzantium, with its theological controversies and its palace politics, seemed to be the sinister caricature of a retrogressive society, and was derided as such by Montesquieu and Voltaire. It was, however, an Englishman, Edward Gibbon, who properly formulated the Enlightenment view of Byzantium as an aspect of Roman decline. Gibbon took the unprecedented step of ignoring the supernatural as an agent in history; as a result, the Christian heroes and institutions of late antiquity were automatically deprived of any special status, and were assessed on a level with the pagan contribution to civilization. The comparison naturally proved unfavorable to the Christians. The best Greek and Latin literature had been written by pagans, and the most stable and tolerant period of imperial rule was the 2nd century AD, when Christianity was still a minority religion. The Christianization of the empire in the 4th century followed a period of military and moral collapse; it coincided with a growth of bureaucracy and "Oriental despotism"; it seemed to promote flabbiness of thought and emptiness of style. Constantine, Eusebius and Athanasius emerged as near villains. Justinian's reign, for all its superficial brilliance, was shown to be a time of internal violence and natural disaster. The decline and fall of the Roman Empire were thus seen as "the triumph of barbarism *and religion*"; the Byzantine Empire was seen as perpetuating some of the worst features of decay, which made its long survival ultimately of less benefit to the world than the barbarian chaos of western Europe.

Gibbon was criticized in his own day for his attitude to Christianity, and in the present century for his treatment of Byzantium (of which more in Chapter 6), which long discouraged interest in the subject. On balance, however, he opened more doors than he closed. In the very conception of his work, he showed that the break-up of the ancient world was a phenomenon no less fascinating than the ancient world itself, and by posing the problem of the "Middle Ages" as something distinct from but overlapping with antiquity he provided a strong motive for future research.

The 19th century and modern scholarship. The 19th century was the age of nationalism. It brought, among other national movements, the Greek War of Independence and the consequent establishment of a modern Greek state. European romantic involvement with Greece (a mixture of enthusiasm and disillusion) and Greek irredentism with regard to Macedonia, Thrace, Constantinople and Asia Minor naturally led to an interest in Byzantium as the medieval phase of Greek history. It was from this point of view that George Finlay wrote a *History of Greece* which is to a large extent a history of the Byzantine Empire, and that Karl Hopf wrote his *Geschichte Griechenlands vom Beginn des Mittelalters,* a book which remains the most comprehensive and original study of the history of the Greek peninsula during the period from the Fourth Crusade (1204) to the Turkish conquest. On the Greek side, the literary historian Paparregopoulos achieved something of an international reputation. The study of medieval Greece was complicated, and on the whole distorted, by the ethnic issue between Greeks and Slavs. From the 1830s, when Fallmerayer raised a storm by declaring that not a drop of Hellenic blood flowed in the veins of the modern Greek people, the racial origins of the European subjects of Byzantium from the 6th century became a major subject of academic controversy. The opposition to the Greek theory of racial purity was joined by the Serbs and Bulgars, who also had designs upon the remaining Ottoman territories in Europe, and behind the Balkan Slavs was imperial Russia. Byzantine studies in Russia were in a sense a product of Russian nationalism. Tsarist expansionism in the eastern Mediterranean, combined with the quest for the cultural and institutional origins of Russia prior to Peter the Great, naturally

The Battle of Navarino (20 October 1827), the decisive naval engagement of the Greek War of Independence against Turkey. The combined British-French-Russian fleet was commanded by Admiral Sir Edward Codrington.

brought Russian intellectuals face to face with Byzantium. Before the Revolution, Russia was at the forefront of studies in Byzantine liturgy, law and agrarian organization.

The 19th century was also the age of Romanticism, and as such brought a fashion for things medieval. Interest in the Crusades inevitably contributed to the discovery of Byzantium, especially in France, where the semi-popular works of Chalandon and Schlumberger brought the subject to a relatively wide public.

The 19th century was, finally, the great age of German Classical philology, and out of this grew the critical study of late Greek texts. Most Byzantine historians are still read in the volumes of a Corpus published at Bonn in the 1820s and 1830s. Towards the end of the century, Karl Krumbacher published what is still the standard survey of Byzantine literature. Krumbacher also contributed to Byzantine studies by inaugurating an annual review devoted exclusively to Byzantinology, the *Byzantinische Zeitschrift*; this remains the standard repertory for all

publications in the field. A learned journal is not in itself the hallmark of a nation's competence in a given area of study, but it does reflect the degree of academic status accorded. Russia was not long in starting its own Byzantine periodical, the *Vizantijskij Vremenik*, but no other regular publications appeared until after World War I, in Greece, Italy, Belgium and Czechoslovakia. France, Austria, Yugoslavia and the United States were not represented until after World War II, and despite the monumental contribution of J. B. Bury (1861–1927) it was not before this decade that Britain acquired its own journal of Byzantine and Modern Greek studies.

Archaeology. The Enlightenment, by drawing a sharp distinction between the Classical and Byzantine worlds, tended to discourage interest in Christian antiquities. As a result, travelers of the period 1750–1850, although generally more observant and analytical than their predecessors, being for the most part men with a scientific or technical training, are not much more informative about Byzantine remains. However, the use of ancient spoils in medieval buildings and the occasional problem of dating or identifying a site frequently earned a mention for the despised monuments of the "Bas-Empire." The accounts of 19th-century travelers are of value, also, in that they

Above: a romantic view of Antioch. An engraving (1840) by W. H. Bartlett of the wall on the west side of the city.

Above right: the narthex of the Church of the Virgin, Asinou, Cyprus. Conservation work on the paintings of the 40 Martyrs of Sebaste and figures of monk saints on the side wall.

represent the most thorough attempts to determine the geography of the ancient world on the basis of surface evidence. In this respect, the records of travelers such as Texier and Ramsay in Asia Minor, Pouqueville and Leake in Greece, are still valuable for the student of the Byzantine provinces.

Despite the 19th-century Gothic revival, western Europeans were slow in coming to appreciate the very different Christian art and architecture of Byzantium. In the early decades of the present century, however, there appeared a number of studies of major Byzantine monuments, with attempts to define patterns and influences in Byzantine taste: in particular one may mention the work of Van Millingen and Ebersolt in Constantinople; of Strygowsky in Syria and Egypt; of Tafrali and Diehl in Thessalonica, and of Gabriel Millet in other parts of Greece and the Balkans. Their publications laid the foundation for the academic and technical study of standing remains, which is now fairly sophisticated.

The record of excavation analysis is less satisfactory.

There has never been a Schliemann, Evans or Carter to win popular recognition for Byzantine archaeology; this and the fact that Byzantinists have only recently begun to ask penetrating questions of excavatable material long inhibited the development of adequate standards and techniques. Byzantine strata are invariably quite near the surface, and this has made them the first to be disturbed by contemporary habitation, or effaced by over-zealous excavators in search of the ancient levels beneath. Even where a late Roman or a "Byzantine" settlement has been the object of excavation, as in several sites in Greece and Yugoslavia, evidence from later than the 6th century has not always been recorded with due sensitivity. During the middle and late Byzantine periods building techniques were poor, spoils were used extensively, and carved inscriptions were rare; thus in the corresponding levels the evidence of a stray coin can be crucial, and the close dating of pottery types is essential. The evidence of building methods in standing monuments whose phases can be dated exactly – one need look no further for an example than Hagia Sophia – has not been used to full advantage. The number of sites where the Byzantine material has been properly recorded or preserved is very limited. In spite of this, advances are discernible. The excavations at Corinth and Athens and the Great Palace of Constantinople have yielded much material for comparison. Those in progress at Prespa and two sites in Istanbul, the Kalenderhane Cami and the Saraçhane, are commendable attempts to analyze the development of complex and virtually undocumented sites, and may do much to make archaeology a fine instrument rather than a blunt weapon in the hands of the Byzantine historian.

Opposite above: a mosaic from the dome of St George's Church, Thessalonica, drawn by Charles Texier and published in his *Byzantine Architecture* (1864). Comparison with the modern photograph (*opposite below*) illustrates the liberties Texier took with his drawing.

Below: the site of the Walker Trust excavation of the Great Palace, Constantinople, from a minaret of the Sultan Ahmed Mosque.

2. The Twilight of the Roman Empire

The crisis of the 3rd century. The fateful words which Septimius Severus addressed to his sons from his deathbed at York in 211 AD, "Enrich the soldiers, ignore everyone else," presaged troubles to come. His empire consisted of a 5,000-mile frontier, protected by nature and some 300,000 professional troops, and the vast rich lands of the interior. These were divided into the territories of innumerable cities, whose local aristocracies administered them and willingly provided the public works and services which distinguished Classical civilization. Two centuries of peace had made the cities large and prosperous and brought a comfortable standard of living under a government which represented a theoretical balance between the emperor, the senatorial aristocracy and the army.

The balance was fatally upset by the reforms of Severus who raised the pay and privileges of the troops while degrading the senate. Soldiers could rise far in the militarized civil service which Severus expanded, and had the right to live with their wives outside the camps, which meant that the frontier legions tended to become a peasant militia with local loyalties, commanded by men risen from the ranks. These reforms, which made the empire more democratic and its administration more despotic,

were a great expense, partly met by harsher tax collection, partly by the dangerous expedient of debasing the currency.

As long as the dynasty of Severus was in power, the frontiers were defended and the loyalty of the troops maintained. In 211 Caracalla, the son of Severus, completed a long process by granting Roman citizenship to all free men, apparently to make them all eligible for taxation. The population was prosperous, as revealed by the abundant construction of baths, theaters, markets and all kinds of public works in the cities, usually in an ornate baroque style. Increasing expense of government, however, coincided with ominous developments outside the frontiers. During the reign of Alexander, the last of the Severi, the decadent Parthians of Persia were replaced by the dynamic and nationalistic Sasanians, and great movements took place among the Germans. The Goths settled near the Black Sea, and tribes as far west as the Rhine, displaced by the migrations, began to harass the empire, which lacked the manpower for active fighting on two fronts.

Disruption began under Maximinus, the first soldier to gain supreme power. His successes with the army – he

Bronze and silver coins to celebrate the millennium of Rome. The obverse legends of these coins struck by Philip I in 248 employ the Classical titles of Emperor, Caesar and Augustus; the reverses show animals destined for the games to celebrate the 1000th anniversary of the founding of the city. British Museum.

Above: the two Augusti, Diocletian and Maximian, portrayed in the serious military attitude of the day. Vatican Library.

Opposite: the civic center of Anemurium, at the southernmost point of Asia Minor. The buildings here shown – odeon, basilica and gymnasium – were part of a grandiose building project of the mid-3rd century. Unfinished at the time of the Persian invasion of 260, they were abandoned, and later converted to new uses.

doubled their pay and defeated the Germans – were matched by troubles with the civilian population. Africa rose in revolt against ruthless tax collection, and though this was suppressed with much bloodshed and destruction, the senate took up arms, and the emperor fell besieging the Roman city of Aquileia. A respite followed during which Philip, an Arab chieftain, celebrated in 248 AD the millennium of Rome with lavish games, the last of their kind, which symbolize the end of the Classical era. He perished the next year in a civil war led by Decius whose successes against the Goths had moved his troops to proclaim him emperor. A sinister process had begun by which each army felt capable of seizing power; in the civil wars which followed, the frontier was denuded just when pressure on it was strongest.

The nadir of the empire came in the reign of Gallienus, who assumed sole power after the two greatest disasters yet seen. In 251 AD Decius was killed and his army destroyed by the Goths who ravaged the Balkans, and in 260 Valerian was taken captive by the Persians, who had sacked Antioch, the greatest city of the east. At the same time, the plague struck, and decimated the population for two decades. Under Gallienus the Persians ravaged the east, German tribes devastated Asia Minor, the Balkans and Gaul, and innumerable usurpers gained ephemeral power as the provinces, seeing the inability of Rome to defend them, took matters into their own hands. Most important was Postumus who ruled a separate empire of Gaul, Britain and Spain from his capital at Trier, seat of his senate and consuls. In the east, Roman fortunes were saved by Odaenathus, sheikh of Palmyra, but after his murder, his ambitious wife Zenobia threw off allegiance and seized the provinces from Asia Minor to Egypt.

In this crisis Gallienus made a reform which was to have permanent effect. Since defense by stationary legions had failed, he created a new army at Milan to defend Italy. This force was of cavalry protected by the scale armor of the Persians, armed with lances and German long swords and bearing barbarian standards in the shape of dragons, a model which was followed for centuries. Barbarians, especially Germans, entered the army in large numbers, and senators were excluded from military command, a prohibition which reduced the senate to an influential leisured class, put the army into the hands of professional soldiers and encouraged the separation of civil and military careers.

Gallienus was murdered in 268 AD, but the effect of

his work was seen in the successes of the harsh but efficient Illyrian emperors who followed. Claudius crushed the Goths, and Aurelian reunited the empire, by defeating Tetricus, the last Gallic emperor, and Zenobia. Both adorned his triumph and were settled comfortably in Italy. The walls of Rome were the work of Aurelian, as was the abandonment of the no longer defensible trans-Danubian province of Dacia. Unity was also sought through religion, by making the Unconquered Sun, god of the armies, the focus of universal loyalty, while the emperor himself became a more awesome and remote figure, surrounded by elaborate ceremonial.

The successors of Aurelian, Probus who defeated the Germans in Gaul and worked to restore the provinces, and Carus who chastized the Persians, maintained an implacable and competent government. As the Roman army returned from Persia, Numerian the son of Carus was found dead, apparently murdered by the praetorian prefect, who mounted the podium at Nicomedia to reveal the news. At that moment he was suddenly run through by one of his officers, Diocletian, whose dramatic avenging of his master's death was an apt prelude to the vast changes he wrought, stamping the image of late antiquity onto the fabric of the empire.

Diocletian and the restoration of order.

When Diocletian came to the throne, he found the empire in internal chaos. The population had been reduced by plague, famine and war, vast tracts of land were deserted, whole provinces lay in ruins, the cities were bankrupt and the currency was worthless. Dominating all this was the instability of the government and the uncontrolled violence of the troops. For ten years Diocletian struggled against the enemies of the state, making expedient and innovative reforms. To counter the Bacaudae in Gaul, he appointed a co-emperor, and to face the revolt of Carausius, who set up an independent state in Britain, and the invasions of the Persians, created two subordinate emperors. After victories on all fronts, the empire enjoyed peace which it had not seen for half a century, and the emperor, having finished his work, could retire peacefully in 305. The last years of his reign, however, were marked by a different battle – against the Christians, who refused to accept his universal religion of Jupiter and Hercules. The persecutions lasted a decade but succeeded only in strengthening the Church by the blood of its martyrs.

Diocletian took measures to ensure that the hard-won peace and stability would last. Security against invasion and revolt was his main goal. Political stability was to be secured by radical reform and multiplication of the government. Two Augusti and two subordinate Caesars now ruled from strategic capitals in east and west. Each had a praetorian prefect in charge of the administration and army supplies, with officers to supervise finance. Subordinate to him were the provincial governors, now over 100 as the provinces were divided to prevent

Above: Aurelian, restorer of the Roman world. This coin, commemorating the reunification of the empire, was nominally of silver, but actually bronze with a thin silver wash. In regularity and workmanship, however, it represented a great improvement over those of earlier reigns. British Museum.

Opposite: a relief of the 4th century in the Trêves Museum showing tax collectors and the payment of tribute money.

concentration of power and ensure responsible government. Most governors had no military command, which was assigned to generals (*duces*), but controlled local justice and finance, and oversaw the cities whose councillors were personally responsible for collection of local taxes, an onerous and undesirable duty. Governorships, like other offices, were usually held for short terms so that they could not become bases for revolt.

These changes involved a vast increase in the size and scope of government and the need for qualified candidates for civil careers, effectively separated from military. The spread of education was thus encouraged, and professors were subsidized by the state. Training usually concentrated on writing and speaking and encouraged the baleful tradition of verbose and vapid rhetoric which was to dominate Greek letters for a millennium. At the same time, the army was doubled in size and the frontier strengthened with new fortresses and legions.

The reforms demanded an immense increase in revenue, for which the state was prepared to sacrifice the interests of the individual. An attempt to stop inflation by the introduction of new coinage followed by a harsh decree fixing the price of all goods came to nothing, but the state suffered little, for the bulk of its revenues and expenses were by now in goods rather than money. Collection and guarantee of regular production therefore became essential, and the empire adopted a budget for the first time. Taxes were assessed annually on the basis of a periodic census which recorded people, animals and land, so that accurate calculations of resources could be made for each region, and expenses planned accordingly. The taxes, mostly requisitions in kind, fell heavily on the rural population, but city- and country-dwellers alike were subject to forced labor on public works. To provide supplies and save money, Diocletian also set up a network of state-run factories for armor and weapons.

This system had far-reaching social consequences.

Everyone counted in the census had to have a fixed domicile; to secure the revenues, the government tended to prohibit free movement and to fix the cultivators to the soil. Such compulsion became a fundamental aspect of the state: sons of soldiers had to join the army, producers of essential supplies were organized into hereditary guilds, and elaborate measures were taken to prohibit city councillors or their sons from escaping their obligations.

The spirit of the age was manifested in its arts and buildings, which by their size and number illustrate the peace and prosperity restored by Diocletian. In art the elegance and subtlety of the Classical age collapsed by the mid-3rd century as scenes became crowded and turbulent and the drill replaced the chisel to bring an abstract contrast of dark and light. By the time of Diocletian this yielded to a style which featured a rigid hierarchy of figures with little individuality subordinated to a central scene or person; portraits became abstract personifications of office. In architecture, massive walls and spaces dominated the beholder and directed his gaze, while straight lines and rigid arrangements betrayed the influence of the army. Simplification and order triumphed, seemingly for eternity. The spirit is exemplified by the words of the liturgy, itself, like all the apparatus of Christianity, a product of late antiquity: "as it was in the beginning, is now, and ever shall be." At the same time color enlivened buildings, monuments and sculpture; bright paintings and mosaics covered walls and floors and lent gaudiness to the solemnity.

Superficially the system of Diocletian was a failure. After his abdication Augusti and Caesars fought constantly for almost 20 years, but the vast machinery of government which he had set in motion continued its work and ensured the survival of the empire. Under the rigid surface of hierarchy and compulsion, there was much mobility, through education or the army, and such complexity that many obligations were evaded and corruption was rife. Classical civilization, together with city life and the many benefits it brought, was preserved, however transformed.

Constantine and Christianity. When the Augustus Constantius died in 306 AD, his troops ignored the legitimate Caesar to proclaim his son Constantine emperor. After a long struggle he gained sole power and died peacefully leaving the empire to his sons. Constantine took two fundamental steps which completed the transformation of the Roman world: he adopted Christianity and founded Constantinople. Before the battle which gave him control of Italy in 312, Constantine saw a vision in the sky of a cross with the words "In this sign shalt thou conquer." He adopted the sign, won the battle and henceforth behaved like a Christian. His motives were probably genuine and personal, but by assuming a religion which the state would follow, he behaved like Aurelian or Diocletian, and gained a powerful new weapon as the Church became closely associated with the government.

Constantine intervened in Church affairs, beginning with the problem of the Donatists in Africa and culminating in the Council of Nicaea in 325, where he presided. His actions naturally had great influence and promoted conversion to Christianity. They were reflected in his new residence—Rome officially remained the capital for a time – where churches rather than temples were constructed. In choosing the site of Constantinople, he was guided by a vision of Christ, the precedent of Diocletian who had ruled from nearby Nicomedia, and strategic considerations; the water and walls which surrounded the city were destined to preserve the empire through its worst crises. The city itself was to be the center of the civilized world for 11 centuries, the meeting point of eastern and western cultures, and remains to this day the principal see of the Orthodox Church.

Adulation of Christian writers has obscured the picture of Constantine who was also responsible for military and financial reforms. Following Gallienus, he established a large field army quartered in the interior; it soon became the most important defense of the empire. He increased the bureaucracy, made extravagant gifts to the Church (which, however, provided many valuable social services) and raised taxes. Although he gained a great windfall by confiscating the accumulated treasures of the temples, expenses grew and inflation raged unchecked. Constantine did, however, establish the stable gold currency which was to last into the Middle Ages. By the end of his reign the government had assumed the shape it would keep for 1,000 years – a despotic Christian state ruled from the east. The west was nevertheless still mostly pagan, the language of the government was Latin, and its extravagance and corruption resulted in inefficiency and weakness.

Julian and paganism. After two of Constantine's sons perished in civil war, the survivor, Constantius II, reunited an empire disturbed by struggles between the Christian sects, which now influenced the highest circles, by the growth and extravagance of the administration, and by Persian and German attacks. The latter were so serious that Constantius appointed his young cousin Julian as Caesar to pacify Gaul. Julian was so successful that his troops raised him to imperial power, and he became sole emperor when Constantius providentially died. In his brief reign Julian did much to root out corruption and extravagance, and even reduced the taxes, but he is best remembered for his attempt to restore paganism to which

he had been converted as a student by the magician and philosopher Maximus of Ephesus. He left the Christians free to fight each other and strengthened paganism along the lines of the Church. Although most of the west was still pagan, he received a chill reception in the east where he spent most of his reign, and his efforts died with him as he fell fighting the Persians.

Julian's successor died after a few months in office, but the machinery of government moved smoothly through the crises, and the army settled on a minor officer, Valentinian, who moved west, leaving his brother Valens to rule the east. Both followed similar policies of fighting corruption, favoring the lower classes in city and country and striving to maintain the manpower of the army. With increased pressure on the frontiers, military service became less attractive, while the government inclined to exempt cultivators from service to maintain the revenue. The problem soon found a partial and disastrous solution.

Valentinian died in 375 AD and was succeeded by his son. In the autumn of 376 the whole nation of the Visigoths appeared on the Danube, begging refuge from a new and terrible enemy, the Huns. Since men were needed for the army, the tribesmen were ferried across the Danube to be settled on imperial territory, but the arrangements were so corruptly mismanaged that the Visigoths broke into

Below left: the battle of the Milvian bridge. A scene from the Arch of Constantine showing his great victory over Maxentius outside Rome in 312.

Below: the vision of Constantine before the battle which gave him control of Italy in 312. A 15th-century mural in the Church of the Holy Cross at Platanistasa, Cyprus.

revolt, soon joined by Ostrogoths and escaped slaves. In 378 Valens hastened to Adrianople to quell the revolt, but instead was killed along with most of his army. With this disaster, the greatest since Decius, the empire entered the age of migrations.

The division of the empire and the fall of the west.

The new emperor Theodosius filled the ranks of the army by ruthless conscription and came to terms with the Visigoths: in exchange for military service, they were allowed to settle in the empire under their own chiefs. This dangerous precedent was satisfactory for the moment because of rebellions in the west, notably that of Maximus who crossed from Britain. Only for the last few months of his reign did Theodosius control the whole empire, which now came to be ruled from Constantinople and to be identified with Orthodox Christianity. The fanaticism of the emperor, abetted by Ambrose of Milan, led to the prohibition of heresy and paganism and the closing of the temples. The state assumed the duty of enforcing the right practices; intolerance became a permanent characteristic, removing the empire still further from its Classical origins.

The 4th century, in spite of repeated troubles, was basically peaceful; commerce and manufacture thrived to produce a spate of construction throughout the empire.

The triumph of Christianity. *Below:* a chapel built in the 4th century over a corner of the abandoned temple of Artemis at Sardis. *Right:* the temple of Aphrodite at Aphrodisias converted into the cathedral, for which the new pavement was laid, and several columns moved. Later, the name of the city was changed to the more acceptable Stauropolis, "City of the Cross."

Basilican churches especially were built in vast numbers, and public buildings were constructed or restored, though in the west, where city life had declined, the prosperity is more evident in rural villas. Problems of maintaining the army and agriculture, however, continued to grow, especially as the empire fell into the hands of feeble rulers, cloistered in their palaces, each ruling half the empire.

Theodosius' closest adviser had been the Vandal Stilicho, to whom the government of the west, nominally ruled by the slothful Honorius, was entrusted. During his supremacy (395–408) massive barbarian migrations struck the empire at a time when relations with Constantinople were hostile. East and west disputed the Balkan provinces, which were being ravaged by the Visigoth Alaric, and when Gildo revolted in Africa and cut off the grain supply of Rome, he received the tacit support of the eastern court. Stilicho managed to drive Alaric and another German horde away from Italy, but the last years of his power saw events which sealed the doom of the west.

In 405 the Ostrogoths ended Roman control north of the Alps and descended on Italy. No sooner were they defeated than, on the last day of 406, the nations of the Vandals, Sueves and Alans crossed the frozen Rhine into Gaul, most of whose troops had been withdrawn to protect Italy. Soon joined by the Burgundians, they ravaged the country for two years before moving into Spain. Roman control was nominally maintained by a usurper, Constantine, who led the legions of Britain to Gaul and Spain until he was finally suppressed by Honorius' general Constantius. Meanwhile Stilicho had been assassinated and Alaric moved on Italy. In 410 the inconceivable happened: Rome itself was taken and plundered by the Visigothic host, the first enemy to capture the city since the Gauls of 390 BC. The repercussions were enormous, and many believed that the end of the world was at hand; the *City of God* by St Augustine was written to exculpate the Christians for the calamity.

The Visigoths eventually moved on Gaul where a series of revolts had broken out. As allies of the empire, together with Constantius, they restored some order in the province, for which they received lands in the south. Constantius soon died to be replaced by Aetius who defended Gaul for a generation of chaos: there were constant troubles between the Germans and their Roman "hosts," exacerbated by violent struggles among the German tribes and unceasing slave and serf revolts. Agriculture suffered terribly, but the province was large and rich, and much survived to contribute badly needed revenues. Gaul became all the more important with the loss of the richest province, Africa, to the Vandals,

who entered it in 429 and within ten years had taken Carthage. Italy was now faced with food shortage as well as the constant threat of the Vandal fleets.

As long as Aetius lived, some control was maintained in Gaul – the Burgundians were crushed in 435, and he even defeated the great attack of Attila in 451 – but the empire rapidly collapsed after his murder in 454. Civil wars and invasions followed; Rome was sacked by the Vandals in 455, they captured Sicily in 467, and little remained under direct rule in Gaul or Spain. A series of generals ruled through puppet emperors until 476 when the German Odoacer deposed Romulus Augustulus and assumed the title of king under the nominal suzerainty of the eastern emperor. The Western Empire was at an end, though Roman forces under Syagrius held out in Gaul for a decade until they succumbed to Clovis the Frank.

Many explanations have been offered for "the fall of the Roman empire" – depopulation, soil exhaustion, climatic change, lead poisoning, lack of precious metals, racial

Galla Placidia. Gold medallion showing the empress whose career illustrates the vicissitudes of the age. Sister of Honorius, she was captured by the Visigoths when they sacked Rome, and married to their king. After finally being returned to Rome, she married the co-emperor Constantius and became regent for her son Valentinian III, dying before the second sack of Rome. Bibliothèque Nationale, Paris.

mixture, Christianity, the barbarians, accident – but no universal answer can be satisfactory unless it also explains why the empire in the east survived for two centuries longer. While some of the alleged causes may be valid – climatic change, for example, could account for the migrations – the real explanation, if there is one, must isolate factors peculiar to the west and determine why the combination of invasion and civil war from which the empire recovered in the 3rd century proved fatal in the 5th.

The west differed from the east in three important respects: resources, social structure and vulnerability. The east had a large and rich population firmly rooted in city life and developed trade and manufacture, while in the west (except for Africa) cities never recovered from the trials of the 3rd century, and a smaller population dwelled on, or under the influence of, large estates, scattered and decentralized. This, as will be seen in the next chapter, is evident from the archaeological record. The immediate cause of disaster was the great and sudden movement of the German tribes against whom the long Rhine and Danube frontier could not be held. As the invasions were compounded by civil war, the state had to strain its resources and use one tribe against another. Meanwhile the loss of provinces, beginning with the Danube and Britain and culminating in Africa, drastically reduced the revenues, as did the settlement of barbarian "allies" who demanded money or land for their services.

Shortage of manpower and revenue was compounded by the social structure of the west. Lacking an effective network of cities, taxes had to be collected from the great landowners whose influence, exercised through the Roman senate, enabled them to escape many of their obligations. In addition they were never willing to surrender *coloni*, on whose existence their revenues depended, for conscription into the army, however critical the situation. As its territory shrank and no alternative source of revenue could be found, the empire had no hope of recovery. Lacking men, money and public spirit, it was remarkably successful to survive as long as it did.

Continuing prosperity in the east. In the east the 5th century was relatively tranquil. Although the Balkan provinces were ravaged by Alaric and ruined by Attila, who also drained vast sums of gold as tribute, the well-populated lands of Asia Minor, Syria and Egypt continued to produce the revenue needed to support the state. Wars with the Persians were spasmodic and inconclusive; only the ravages of the Isaurians in Asia Minor and the nomads and Vandals in Cyrenaica seriously disturbed the peace. Deserts and heavy fortifications protected the eastern frontier, and the walls of Constantinople were an insurmountable obstacle for the northern barbarians.

For the first half of the century the east was ruled by the indolent Arcadius and Theodosius II, dominated by eunuchs, women and ministers of varying competence and honesty. The administration nevertheless functioned, the city councils continued to collect the taxes, the armies remained loyal, and the one attempted coup, by the German Gainas, was easily suppressed. Archaeology, however, suggests that even the east may have been in decline for these years: few large buildings can be dated to the time, inscriptions are rare, and the bronze coinage degenerated to a level which it had not reached even in the 3rd century. The explanation of these phenomena is far from clear, especially because the historical record was preoccupied with the Christian doctrinal differences which wracked the empire. Three Church councils and the determined efforts of the civil authorities could not reconcile the opposing parties, whose quarrels caused lasting bitterness and dissension, especially between the capital and Syria and Egypt.

The latter part of the century saw an improvement, except for an interlude when the Isaurian bandits ruled the empire. A chief called Tarasicodissa gained supreme power under the more acceptable name Zeno because of the need for his warlike and troublesome compatriots. His reign was marked by civil war, by the construction of lavish churches in his mountainous homeland, and by the fall of the west, of which Zeno took advantage by sending off the Ostrogoths to reconquer Italy in his name. His successor, Anastasius, expelled the Isaurians from office and crushed their rebellion, but was less fortunate in the

Attila the Hun. For a short period (c. 445–53) he united the nomads against the Roman Empire and invaded Gaul and Italy, but was defeated by Aetius in 452. Museo della Certosa, Pavia.

Balkans where the Bulgars appeared, in his inconclusive war with Persia, and in religious policy where the old antagonisms continued. Financially, however, the reign of Anastasius saw a great improvement. Extravagance and corruption were curtailed, and a new bronze coinage with clear marks of value was issued, the first good small change, so essential for commerce, in a century. By this time the state also had an adequate gold coinage in three denominations and had begun to assess the taxes in money, except for those which provided supplies for the army. In spite of great expenses, Anastasius could reduce taxes and leave behind a surplus of 300,000 pounds of gold, facts which clearly illustrate the resources available in the east to an efficient government.

Most of the government, however, was hopelessly corrupt, the vast majority of the population sunk in poverty; only vigilance and economy could ensure success. Before considering the reign of Justinian, who made great changes in all realms, it might be well to pause and examine the workings of government and society in late antiquity.

The machinery of government. At the head of the state stood the emperor, a remote figure surrounded by elaborate ceremonial. His despotic power, exercised through innumerable officials, and confirmed by the Church, was tempered by the need for the approval of the army and by the advice of a circle of the highest civil and military officials. A weak emperor might be dominated by his women or the eunuchs of his bedchamber, who had free access to his person, but a strong ruler could leave his impress on the history of the age. The government centered on the emperor and moved with him on campaigns or travels. Its work was carried out by a huge bureaucracy under the praetorian prefect, which, although rigid, complex and overgrown, and notorious for its corruption and love of paperwork, provided the continuity and stability which enabled the empire to survive through crises and change of rulers and administrators.

Much of the work of government was done by governors responsible for provincial administration, finance, justice and public works. Like their superiors, they were mostly amateurs, whose main qualifications were good education and connections. Administrative posts, generally held for short terms, were much sought after as valuable stepping-stones in a career. Appointments, theoretically made by the emperor, were controlled by his ministers, who exacted a high price for their services, which turned into a regular sale of offices. Since salaries were not high, office-holders used all means to regain their investments and to acquire funds to rise to higher office. Corrupt governors were particularly notorious; Euthalius who ruled Lydia in the late 4th century was not unusual: he plundered the province so badly that he was fined 15 pounds of gold by the praetorian prefect. After success-

An Isaurian monastery. The church of Alahan, built during the reign of Zeno, the bandit chief who became emperor, in the remote mountains of his native land.

fully embezzling this sum, he used the fortune he had gained as governor to rise to a distinguished career. Governors usually made illicit gains by misappropriating funds, collecting excess tax, and especially by the sale of justice. On the other hand, because they needed to gain a good name in the province to advance, they often built or began great public works, and worked to gain the favor of influential provincial senators.

The influence of rich landowners, which permeated the government, was particularly evident in the system of justice. Most cases were heard by the governors who would not wish or dare to offend anyone of higher rank.

Local magnates had the right to enter the governor's residence and to sit with him on the bench; they frequently interfered for themselves or their clients. Appeals, to the vicars, prefects or emperor, were long and expensive and cases often dragged on for years.

The machinery of government rested ultimately on the cities, whose councillors, called decurions, maintained the roads, post and public buildings, levied recruits for the army and labor for public works, and, most important, collected the taxes, for whose payment they were personally and collectively responsible. These obligations destroyed the spirit which had once produced willing candidates and led those eligible to seek every means of escape – the army, holy orders or higher rank – leaving fewer and generally poorer members. The government strove constantly to maintain the councils, but was obliged frequently to interfere in the cities through the governors or special officials.

Economic conditions. The main concern of the state was the taxes, which fell almost entirely on the rural population, for the economy of the empire was based on agriculture, with trade far less important. Although some products, such as clothing, pottery and marble, gained wide circulation, most trade was on a small local scale; production was generally carried out in cities or estates by craftsmen who sold their own goods. The state, which requisitioned and shipped its own needs, bypassed trade altogether, and foreign trade, essentially in luxury goods, was relatively minor.

The taxation system of Diocletian was maintained through the period. It was not progressive and fell heavily on the small cultivator whose labor ensured production on his own plot or on vast estates worked by tenants. Rates were high: free farmers paid about a third of their crop, and bound tenants about half. Only a portion of this, however, reached the central government, for opportunities for peculation were enormous. The decurions were ruthless extortionists, governors did not hesitate to take an illicit share of the revenues, the agents of the treasuries, who supervised tax collection, had to be specifically forbidden from tampering, and other agents, who audited the accounts, profited from blackmail and bribery. The vast complexity of the financial system, in which three separate treasuries handled different revenues and disbursements, did little to ensure its efficiency.

The rapacity of officials was a major problem which effected more than the revenues. Romanus, count of Africa under Valentinian, provided the most notorious example when he refused to intervene to help the city of Leptis, ravaged by nomad barbarians, because the citizens failed to bribe him. As successive attacks followed, the city in vain sent delegations to the court, where Romanus' influence protected him. He was finally arrested but escaped punishment through the intervention of a powerful general. Leptis never recovered from the devastation.

The taxpayers were basically peasants, most of them

Right: the 1100th year of Rome, coins of Constans II. These show the great changes which had taken place in a century. The emperor is now styled "Our Lord," a title appropriate to a master of slaves. The reverses show the emperor spearing a fallen barbarian, and a soldier leading a captive from a burning hut. The legend may be roughly translated as "Happy days are here again." British Museum.

Opposite: art and technology. Representation of a water mill, one of the major technological advances of the age, which enabled a smaller population to maintain a high level of production, in a floor mosaic of the Great Palace of Constantinople.

leading a marginal existence. Labor was apparently short – every effort was made to tie cultivators to the land and recover those who had fled – and it seems that the population never recovered from the troubles of the 3rd century, perhaps because the peasants were too poor to raise children. Their burden was made especially intolerable by the need to support a great number of unproductive consumers – the populations of Rome and Constantinople, the senatorial order, the army, the civil service and the Church. Some of their work, however, may have been lightened by technological progress, such as the increasing use of the watermill to grind flour, which might enable a smaller workforce to produce an adequate supply of food.

Social conditions. The urban population, larger in the east than the west, formed a small portion of the total. Rome and Constantinople had perhaps half a million people each, Alexandria about half that, and Antioch somewhat fewer. Other cities were small by modern standards but were lavishly decorated and provided considerable services for their inhabitants. City dwellers had long since lost any political rights, but could make their opinion felt through riot or peaceful acclamation. This rhythmic shouting, often managed by professional claques, was the order of the day: the people in the hippodrome of Constantinople used it to communicate with the emperor; meetings of the senate and councils of the Church featured it. Individual opinion blended into the larger and simpler voice of the crowd, an image of the age seen also in the art.

The acclamations often reflected the violence and brutality of a time when torture and burning alive were routine, at least for those who had no rank or office. The Church as well as the urban mob provides examples, of which the most gruesome perhaps took place during the Council of Ephesus in 449. The assembled fathers shouted "As he divides, let him be divided" against an offending bishop who maintained the separate natures of the Father and Son, and tore him to pieces.

The people of late antiquity were highly religious and superstitious. Astrology, divination and magic had a great vogue and influence in the highest circles. Julian the Apostate was converted to paganism on hearing of a miracle in which a statue of Hecate was made to smile and the torches in its hands to burst into flame. More notorious was a plot under Valens in which the conspirators asked an apparatus like a Ouija board who the next emperor would be. When it responded with the letters THEO, they believed that it had named one of their number, Theo-

dore, who was apprehended, confessed under torture and was executed. The government then showed its faith in divination by carrying out a great persecution of magicians and philosophers. Ironically the machine was right, for the next emperor was Theodosius.

Christianity contained many elements of the supernatural, and wonder-working holy men, usually monks on the fringes of the established Church, gained tremendous influence in the country. Religion was the active consolation of the whole population, always conscious of a world beyond the present. The Church resembled the state with its patriarchs, its metropolitans in provincial capitals and bishops in each city, its administrative bureaucracy, courts and vast land holdings. Like the state, it provided public services – hospitals, poorhouses, old age homes and hostels – and its policies and doctrines stirred the profoundest emotions, accounting for much sedition and disunity as people felt their future life threatened by erroneous doctrine.

Christian, pagan and Jew were all protected by some 650,000 troops, over half in the east, commanded by masters of the foot and horse directly subordinate to the emperor. More than half the army were frontier guards, settled in forts and used for delaying the enemy until the smaller but superior field armies, billeted in the cities, could come into action. The soldiers were raised by conscription from the rural population (except slaves and bound serfs) and by hereditary service. But great numbers of barbarians were also employed and the empire never hesitated to use diplomacy or bribes for its defense. The troops, given regular salaries and special donatives, enjoyed a higher standard of living than most of the peasantry.

Society as a whole was remarkably uniform: the educational system infused the same culture everywhere, cities had the same kind of buildings, similar villas and villages adorned the countryside. Greek and Latin were the predominant languages, universal among the educated classes, but many in the east spoke only Syriac or Coptic, and Celtic was widespread in the west. All the people, however, thought of themselves as Romans and shared the benefits of the transformed Classical culture. In the east the political situation remained stable until the time of Justinian when exceptional strains caused serious changes, the culmination of earlier developments and reflection of the personality of the ruler.

The reign of Justinian. Justinian was the nephew of an Illyrian peasant; he rose high in the army and chanced to become emperor. He was proud of his Latin language and obsessed with the ideal of the Roman Empire. A hard

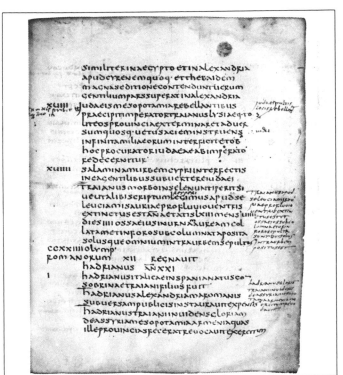

Opposite: courtyard of the palace of the metropolitan archbishop of Caria at Aphrodisias, the provincial capital. The great resources of the Church were well displayed here as in other major cities.

Right: the tradition of learning. A manuscript of the chronicle of Jerome, written in Italy in the mid-5th century, with additions and corrections by a slightly later hand. Bodleian Library, Oxford.

Below: a Syrian village in the 5th century. In the foreground, a large monastery with its orchard; behind, the village houses of stuccoed stone. The whole is typically surrounded by a wall and roughly illustrates the life of a great part of the population. From H. C. Butler, *Princeton Expedition to Syria* (1919).

worker who took little sleep and paid great attention to detail, he chose his ministers and generals well and aimed to restore the glories of Rome and build for posterity. Justinian was assisted in his work by his wife Theodora, a former actress and prostitute, daughter of a bear-keeper in the hippodrome, whose powerful character lent a strong moral tone to the regime.

The emperor also relied on his praetorian prefect, John of Cappadocia, whose ruthless exaction of the taxes supported Justinian's projects but provoked a disastrous riot. The Blues and the Greens, the popular factions around whom the races in the hippodrome were organized, united in a sedition which burned large parts of the center of Constantinople and was quelled only by the determination of Theodora and the resolute action of the general Belisarius whose troops massacred 30,000 of the rioters. After this explosion of the safety valve which linked emperor and people, the population of Constantinople remained quiet for generations. A tangible reminder of the revolt is the church of St Sophia, built to replace the earlier cathedral which was destroyed.

The reign is perhaps most famous for the ambitious campaigns in which Justinian hoped to restore the Roman Empire. Taking advantage of the decay of the barbarian states, his armies under Belisarius quickly conquered Africa, Sicily and Italy, but the initial successes were followed by revolts and long wars which ruined the newly won provinces. Parts of Spain were also taken, and imperial supremacy in the Mediterranean assured.

Great changes were made in the administration to increase efficiency and reduce corruption. Codification of the Roman law in 529 was a monumental achievement, but most of the reforms were ephemeral. A mass of legislation early in the reign struck at sale of offices, regulated morals, and reformed provincial administration, but no regular system was created. Municipal life reached a new level of decay as the effort to maintain the councils was finally abandoned and administration entrusted to the bishops and landowners with frequent supervision and interference from the governors. By recognizing the supremacy of the Church and the countryside, Justinian finally put an end to the ancient municipal autonomy which had become meaningless, and bishops assumed the predominant role in the cities which they were to maintain through the Middle Ages. Urban life was generally in decay, as cities were almost entirely

Justinian (*opposite*) and Theodora (*above*). The son of the peasant and the successful prostitute who dominated the history of the 6th century, portrayed surrounded by courtiers in the church of San Vitale in Ravenna.

replaced by small fortresses in the west and suffered a great diminution in their resources elsewhere as the demands of the government increased. Especially destructive was the plague of 542 which ravaged the empire for a generation and decimated the population.

Another ancient tradition came to an end as the emperor, persecuting heresy and paganism, closed the philosophical schools of Athens, though leaving pagans to teach in Alexandria. Orthodoxy was everywhere enforced, but the triumphant Church had a hard master in Justinian who actively participated in theological debates and exercised the same autocracy over the Church as he did over the state.

The ambitions of the reign were reflected in the building program which has left its traces throughout the Mediterranean. St Sophia is its greatest accomplishment, but the churches of Ravenna, Ephesus and Jerusalem were also splendid, and a vast network of fortifications along the Danube and eastern frontiers represented a major effort to bring security and prosperity to the provinces. That work was only partially successful; although Egypt and Syria flourished, the Balkans were constantly ravaged, and much of Asia Minor was in turmoil from banditry, while the new western provinces were exhausted by the wars.

The extravagance of buildings and conquests soon exhausted the immense reserves left by Anastasius. Little profit came from the conquests, and the state only remained solvent by increasing taxes and the severity of their collection, and by eliminating the drain of corruption as far as possible. The peasantry, on whom the burden still rested, did not cease to suffer oppression and misgovernment which provoked serious revolt in some areas.

Justinian succeeded to some extent in restoring the empire; at his death, Italy, Sicily, Africa and part of Spain were again Roman, but the cost had been enormous. The empire nevertheless had the resources for the conquests, the buildings and for maintaining its own against the Persians until it was drastically weakened by the plague. After that armies were far smaller – only 150,000 men defended the whole empire, and far more reliance had to be put on barbarians and diplomacy. The state became relatively impoverished and monumental building was at a standstill.

The end of antiquity. The work of Justinian collapsed soon after his death in a new movement of peoples. In 568 the Lombards descended on Italy and quickly overran the north; revolts of the Moors in Africa reduced Roman control to a network of small forts; the Avars moved into the Hungarian plain and launched devastating attacks on the Balkans and Greece where their allies the Slavs came to settle; and a new long war with Persia began. Solvency could only be maintained by drastic reductions of expenses, many of them in the army.

Maurice made a serious attempt to save the situation. The Persian war was brought to a successful conclusion after a revolution put a Roman ally on the throne, Africa was pacified, and a new government set up there and in Italy, in which supreme officers called exarchs controlled both civil government and army, but the cities of Italy were already devastated and depopulated from the constant wars. The threat of the Avars especially preoccupied Maurice who launched a series of attacks, but the needs of economy forced him to request the troops to spend the winter beyond the Danube. This provoked a revolt led by Phokas, Maurice was deposed and executed, and within a few years the whole fabric of the empire collapsed.

The short reign of Phokas saw the beginning of unparalleled disasters. The Balkans and Greece were overrun and removed from imperial control. The Persian Chosroes, posing as the avenger of Maurice, led his forces across the frontier and within a few years had added Syria, the Holy Land and Egypt to his domains, and so devastated Asia Minor that it never recovered. To mark his triumph, he carried off the True Cross from Jerusalem, and many thought that the end of the world was at hand. In a sense they were right, for the Classical Mediterranean civilization was never to recover. Phokas was soon murdered and succeeded by Heraclius who in a series of brilliant campaigns defeated the Persians and regained the eastern provinces, only to see them fall within a decade to a new and more deadly enemy, the Arabs. By the end of the century, their conquests severed the southern and eastern shores of the Mediterranean from the Classical civilization which had encompassed them for a millennium.

The empire, left with Asia Minor, fragments of the Balkans and of Justinian's conquests, entered a new era of its existence. The rich variety of late antiquity, the Roman Empire which stretched across the Mediterranean, the city life on which its civilization and organization were based, all came to an end as the Byzantine age began.

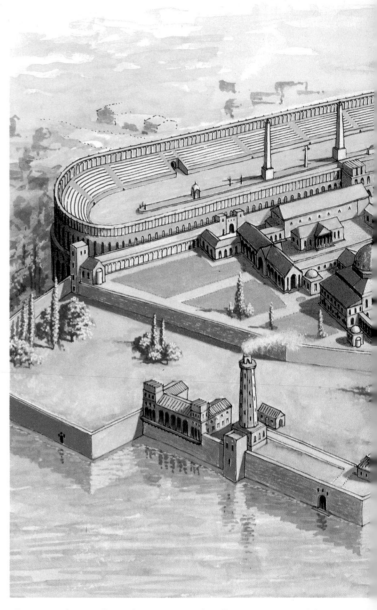

Above: the Great Palace of Constantinople. The nerve center of the empire, this great complex of buildings consisted of palaces, reception rooms, offices and churches; the hippodrome, senate house, main square and cathedral were adjacent. All were extensively restored by Justinian after the Nika revolt. After Vogt.

Opposite: the collapse of antiquity. A statue of Victory lying in the sands of North Africa at Leptis Magna.

Estates and Villas

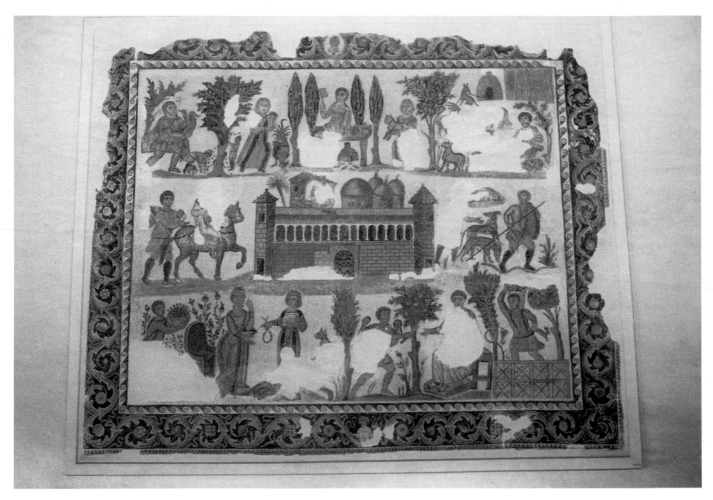

One of the striking characteristics of late antiquity was the growth of large landed estates, a development encouraged by the social and economic conditions of the age, and by the expansion of the government. A vast new ruling class was created which grew rich through government service, and especially from the opportunities of corruption which it offered. This wealth was most commonly invested in the land, resulting in the expansion of existing estates and the creation of new ones.

Large holdings were especially important in the west, notably in Gaul, where the troubles of the 3rd century had dealt a fatal blow to city life and an insecurity which encouraged the peasantry to move from scattered farms and settlements to clustered villages on or near great estates. Those who had capital bought up vast tracts of land, and preferred to live on them, far from the crowded and squalid towns. Such estates tended to predominate in the local economy and to become centers of production for such goods as clothing, tools and pottery. As the towns declined and the estates grew more self-sufficient, whole regions became economically decentralized.

The economic foundation of the empire was agriculture; the well-being of the state depended on revenues raised from the peasants who worked the land. Although independent smallholders survived in all areas, the majority of the peasantry was reduced to serfdom, to become *coloni* who had no right to sell their property or to move from the land, and who were under fixed obligations to the state and the landlord.

The peasants, like the landlords, lived on estates whose

focal point was the villa. Most of these naturally were large farmhouses, but many became complex buildings of great luxury. In the west they were frequently surrounded by dependent buildings for housing, production and storage, but in the east, with the continued flourishing of city life, absentee landlords were common, so that lavish mansions in the cities are found more often than rural villas. Archaeology has revealed great numbers of villas of all types, to provide an important insight into the social and economic conditions of the day.

Above: a working villa: Mungersdorf near Cologne in the 4th century. The main farmhouse (*below*) was of a standard type with a gallery on the facade. Before it, a garden; to the left, a barn; next to the house, a workshop, with stables on the right. Behind, dwellings for the workers, a sheepfold, a pigsty, a tall barn and sheds. The whole complex represents a substantial and probably self-sufficient farm; the walled section contained about ten acres. Reconstructions after H. Mylius.

Opposite: life on a great estate. This 4th-century mosaic from Carthage shows the villa of a certain Julius. The house in the center is fortified with a heavy wall and towers; the main apartments are behind the veranda on the first floor, with a domed bath house behind them. To the left and right, scenes of the lord hunting. Above, *coloni* bring offerings to the lady of the manor, seated on a bench in a park by the hen house; on the left, children gather olives; on the right, the *colonus* herds his flock. The reed hut in the background is a typical tenant-farmer's house. Bardo Museum.

Opposite: the lord of the manor at Piazza Armerina in Sicily. The elderly and serious figure leaning on his staff of authority has been variously identified, sometimes as the Emperor Maximinus who abdicated with Diocletian in 305. In this scene he is engaged in meditation while his two armed guards attend to the transport of captured game in ox carts. This forms part of a mosaic over 60 meters long in the corridor before the audience chamber.

Top: a villa of great luxury: Montmaurın in southern France. Built in the early 4th century to succeed structures destroyed by the Germans around 276, the villa was occupied until it was burned by the Vandals in 408. The semicircular entrance court enclosed a pagan shrine, a common phenomenon, though other villas included Christian chapels. Behind, a peristyle with waiting rooms, dining rooms and kitchens, gave access to a third court which contained the summer house with tanks for keeping fish alive until they were eaten. The walls of the main rooms were covered with marble or painted to resemble it. The baths (*above*) were adjacent on the left, the work buildings further away.

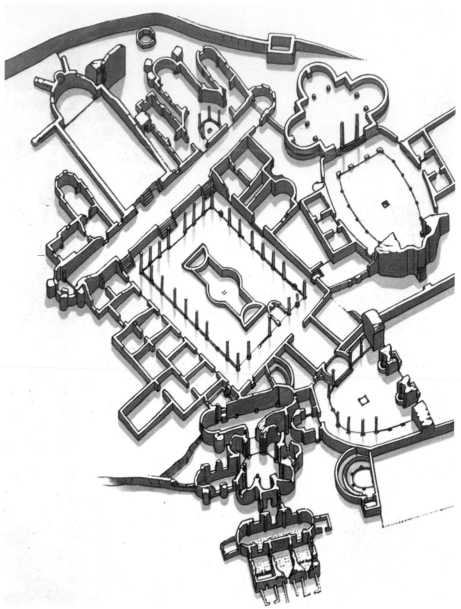

Left: the early 4th-century palace of Piazza Armerina in Sicily. This villa or hunting lodge, one of the most grandiose in the empire, perhaps belonged to a Roman senator. It covers more than three acres, and its floors were decorated with over an acre of excellent mosaics. The rooms are hieratically arranged. Visitors entered through the semicircular vestibule on the lower right, then passed through the great colonnaded garden flanked by living quarters, to the apsed audience hall. Each level was higher than the preceding. To the right of the great hall, private apartments with bedrooms and dining room, and on the right of the garden, a ceremonial wing with an oval court and triple dining room. A suite of baths stands near the entrance. The whole, reminiscent of the villa of Hadrian at Tivoli, represents the last of a long line of open country villas; the future was with fortification. After Gismondi.

Below left and opposite: pastimes of the rich. Hunting scenes from the mosaics at Piazza Armerina.

Left: the palace of Diocletian in Dalmatia as seen today. During the Slavic invasions of the 6th and 7th centuries, the heavy walls of the palace provided refuge for the local population, and a town grew up within them. The area within the walls, 7½ acres, sheltered a population of 3,200 in 1926, and gives an idea of the appearance of many of the towns of the late empire.

Below: the model clearly shows the plan of the vast fortified villa where the Emperor Diocletian retired in 305. The complex was divided like a camp by two main streets, both colonnaded. That running from the north separated the two large blocks of quarters for the troops and staff, and ended in a square facing the great audience chamber. West of the square was a temple of Zeus with a courtyard, and east, the domed octagonal mausoleum of the emperor, whose private apartments, invisible from the outside, were in the lower left quadrant. The plan reflects the military regularity which guided Diocletian's reorganization of the empire. Mostra Augustea, Rome.

Right: the villa at Ephesus. The plan shows a luxurious establishment above the theater at Ephesus, on one of the highest points of the city. It features a peristyle some 30 meters square, with salons, bedrooms and dining rooms around. The house included an apsed reception room, a heated bath and a chapel. *Below:* murals decorating the bath house are still visible today.

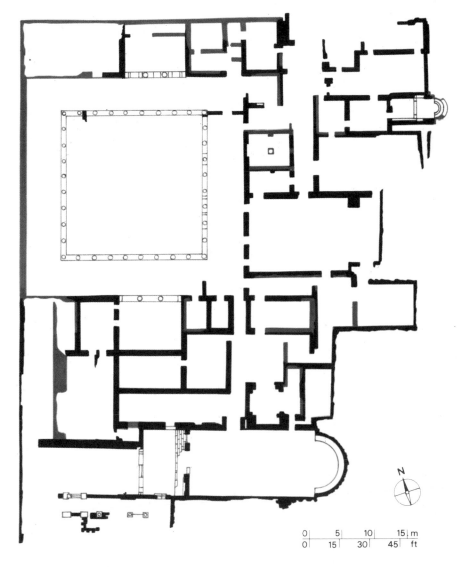

0 5 10 15 m
0 15 30 45 ft

Left: a similar building at Aphrodisias, with two colonnaded courtyards, one of which contained a pool. Such large dwellings were rare in the cities, where most people lived in apartments.

Below: problems of estate management: an Egyptian document of c. 350. Letter from a manager of the imperial estates to the commander of the local garrison informing him that the governor has authorized the manager to employ a detachment of troops to collect the taxes from the imperial lands; the prefect is requested to furnish the troops. Egyptians were especially notorious for their reluctance to pay their taxes, and here, as elsewhere, the government resorted to the strongest forms of coercion to ensure the revenues. Difficulties such as these gradually led the state to prefer indirect tax collection through landlords. British Library.

3.The Monuments of Late Antiquity

The history of late antiquity, a detailed and vivid mosaic of events and personalities, lacks the background of physical remains. They can provide a deeper comprehension of the conditions in which the people lived and the events happened, and of the variety which the late antique world offered in buildings, patterns of settlement and styles of life. The following section will consider the monuments of the Roman Empire from the 3rd through the 6th centuries, beginning in the northwest and proceeding geographically through western Europe, North Africa, the Balkans and the Near East, to end in Egypt.

Late Roman Britain. The remote and relatively undeveloped island of Britain flourished in late antiquity, when peace was secured on the northern frontier by the campaigns of Severus and Constantius, and on the coasts by the fortresses of Carausius. Only in 367 AD, when Picts and Scots descended from the north while Franks and Saxons attacked the shores, was the prosperity interrupted. In the last decades of the 4th century, as troops were withdrawn by usurpers for ventures on the continent, the island was left defenseless at a time when the empire was reeling under Germanic attack and in 410 Honorius had to advise

Previous page: the monastery of Alahan. Almost perfectly preserved except for the timber roof, this 5th-century basilica is noted for its elegant construction.

Above: a pagan sanctuary above the river Severn. The shrine of Nodens, a god of hunting with curative powers, built after 364. His temple stands within the enclosure; the sick, hoping for advice in dreams, would sleep in the long building behind. After Liversidge.

Opposite: London in the 3rd century. The rectangular street pattern with the forum and basilica in the center are typically Roman, but the timber construction and thatched roofs show native traditions.

Below: Porchester Castle. A fort of the Saxon Shore built at the head of Portsmouth harbor as part of the Roman coastal defenses.

the Britons to look to their own defense. Direct Roman rule ended, but the walled cities survived for some decades to maintain a semblance of Roman culture until they gradually succumbed to the Anglo-Saxons.

Because of the density of subsequent occupation and continuous habitation of most sites, Britain is not covered with spectacular ancient remains, but enough survives to reveal clearly the culture the Romans brought and the measures they took to protect it. The most imposing remains are the nine fortresses of the so-called Saxon Shore, a chain stretching from Norfolk to Hampshire, mostly constructed or rebuilt by Carausius. The most interesting is probably Richborough with its different stages of construction, and the most scenic Porchester, where the well-preserved walls of the rectangular fortress rise direct from the sea. Its walls, of the neatly cut stone and courses of brick typical of the age, form a square of some 600 feet with round towers to protect the barracks and depots inside.

Urban life, one of the great benefits which the Romans brought, had also to be defended; most of the cities, protected at first by earthworks, acquired stone walls in the 3rd century and more elaborate fortifications with bastions for artillery towards the end of Roman rule. With the notable exception of London, the cities were small, with an area of 100 acres or less: most of them prospered in the 4th century. The excavations of Verulamium (St Albans) reveal a typical development: the 3rd century saw little building, but Constantius and his successors did extensive work, and large private houses were constructed through the 4th century and maintained well into the 5th. Similarly, Aquae Sulis (Bath), a small town walled in late antiquity, saw extensive remodeling in its curative baths.

Because of the predominance of agriculture in Britain as elsewhere, remains of large farmhouses or villas are frequently encountered. Their growth in the 4th century, when the villa system extended into the north, and when many individual villas were expanded and vast numbers of mosaic floors of varying quality were added, shows the prosperity of British agriculture. The countryside was also dotted with isolated homesteads and villages and with sanctuaries to the pagan gods, for in the western provinces loyalty to the ancient beliefs lasted long among the country dwellers, the *pagani*, from whom our word "pagan" is derived. Traces of Christianity are correspondingly rare; a notable example is the chapel with wall paintings built into the villa at Lullingstone in Kent.

Gaul. Britain provides a striking contrast with the rich provinces of Gaul which stretched from the Rhine to the Pyrenees. The country was far more developed, but suffered more severely from the barbarian invasions. In the

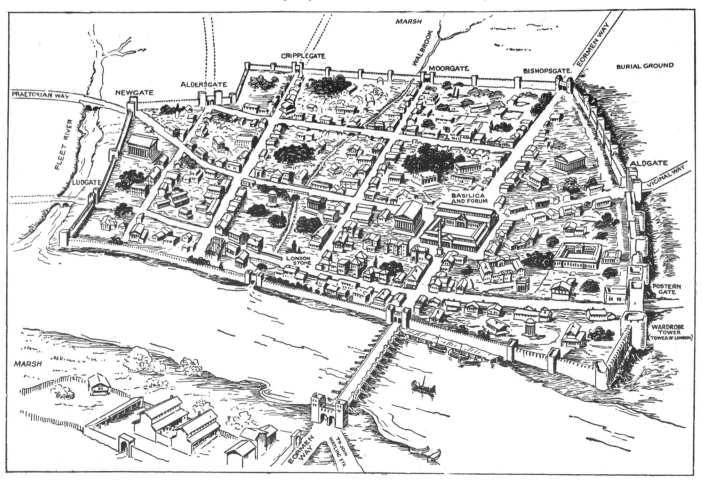

250s and again in 276 AD Gaul, which had known only peaceful prosperity for two centuries, was overrun by the Franks and Alamanni from beyond the Rhine; in the intervening years, the independent state of Postumus provided adequate protection. The attacks destroyed most of the cities, and left a dangerous legacy of dispossessed peasants and runaway slaves who, calling themselves Bacaudae ("the valiant"), infested the countryside.

By the time of Constantius and his son Constantine, who spent many years in Gaul, order was restored and lasted for half a century until civil war provided the occasion for another devastating onslaught. The successes of the young Caesar Julian against this attack resulted in his proclamation as emperor at Paris, whose strategic location he was the first to appreciate. The importance of Gaul continued to increase with the pressure on the frontiers, and from 365 to 375 AD the capital of the west was in the province, at Trier. By the end of the century, however, Gaul faced the same problems as Britain when troops were withdrawn either by pretenders or by the central government needing to protect itself against the Goths. In the winter of 406 a vast horde of Germans crossed the Rhine, and this time there was no one to drive them out. For several decades an uneasy equilibrium was maintained between the Romans and their new German neighbors, who were settled on the land as "allies" of the empire. Gradually, however, the German pressure increased as Rome became ever weaker, so that by 475 the south had fallen to the Visigoths, and in 486 Clovis the Frank took over the last Roman territories in the north.

The abundant and impressive remains of late antique Gaul reflect its wealth and importance, as well as the vicissitudes it suffered. Most of the cities were obliterated in the invasions of the 3rd century and never recovered, being reduced to small towns and fortresses defended by walls made from the ruins of their proud buildings and monuments. The reduction implies a considerable decline in population, the natural consequence of decades of invasion and revolt, famine and plague. Three cities, however, provide notable exceptions to this bleak picture: the imperial residences of Arles, Cologne and Trier.

Cities of Gaul. Constantine spent the first part of his reign in Arles, the "little Rome of Gaul"; Constantius II celebrated the 30th anniversary of his reign there; and under Honorius, when the northern frontier collapsed, it became the capital of Gaul. The most notable traces of this distinguished history are the large bath of Constantine near the Rhône and a unique grain factory outside the city. Constantine also carried out extensive work at Cologne, for long the greatest city of the frontier. He rebuilt the palace on the Rhine, and constructed the bridge across the river and a strong fortress on the opposite side as a bridgehead against the Germans. In the same period a small shrine arose over the grave of some local martyrs; by the end of the century it had been expanded into the

A late antique factory: the mill near Arles. Sixteen wheels in two parallel mill races turned millstones to grind enough flour for 80,000 people; an example of the advanced technology of the day.

church of St Severinus, which has remained in use until the present.

The site of the most imposing Roman remains north of the Alps is Trier, the capital of Postumus, and of the whole Western Empire in the late 4th century. The buildings which survive from the time show the splendor with which the government adorned its capital cities, and provide a remarkable contrast with other cities of Gaul. Unlike them, Trier is surrounded by walls of the 3rd century or earlier which encompass the whole area of the Classical city; they include a monumental gate, the Porta Nigra, which may date from the 4th century. Within the walls, Classical buildings, baths and the amphitheater were restored and several great structures were added.

The most grandiose were the imperial baths of the time of Constantius or Constantine, one of the largest in the empire, with the usual complement of hot and cold baths, swimming pools and a colonnaded exercise ground. It was, however, never completed, but converted into a palace, perhaps for the praetorian prefect, in the time of Valentinian. The main imperial palace is represented by the surviving Basilica, next to which stood the cathedral, a double church of two basilicas side by side, of the time of Constantine. Near the river stood two long warehouses, each almost as large as the Basilica, built in the time of Valentinian. All the structures mentioned are on a gigantic scale, quite unlike anything else to be found in the western provinces, and illustrate the concentration of resources in a capital, often to the detriment of smaller towns.

Rural Gaul. Although the cities generally declined, the rich in the countryside maintained a high standard of refinement and luxury. There are many remains of villas in Gaul, ranging from simple farmhouses to huge and extravagant mansions. Of the latter, the most famous is at

The Porta Nigra at Trier, a monumental gate which may date from the 4th century.

Chiragan on the Garonne south of Toulouse, where the buildings cover $7\frac{1}{2}$ acres. The main house contained dozens of rooms built around colonnaded courtyards in the Mediterranean style, baths, fountains, pools, formal gardens and a summerhouse. In addition, rows of other buildings included dwellings for the workers, stalls for the animals, workshops and barns. This luxurious establishment was a working and probably self-sufficient farm. Other palatial villas are to be found all over Gaul, especially in the Moselle region where the imperial establishments, as at Welschbillig and Konz, are impressive.

The bulk of the population consisted of an impoverished peasantry. Many lived on the estates in a state of virtual serfdom; others had small houses, isolated or clustered in villages. Small settlements tended to occur in forests or on land too poor to support great estates; many of them, particularly in the Vosges, were destroyed in the 3rd century.

The rural settlements often centered on small pagan temples, such as were frequently to be found on estates. As in Britain, there were also numerous rural sanctuaries, with provision for pilgrims and cures; a notable example was excavated at Pesch near Bonn. Paganism prevailed, until 375 AD when the intolerantly orthodox regime of Gratian moved in on the attack and supported the activities of St Martin of Tours, who succeeded in Christianizing most of the countryside.

Late antique remains of a different kind are to be found all along the frontiers of the Rhine and upper Danube. The work of the Tetrarchy and of Constantine is especially evident from Cologne to Regensburg in the construction of numerous fortresses and town walls.

Hispania. The provinces of Hispania (modern Spain and Portugal) have a history and monuments similar to those of Gaul, though known in far less detail. Extreme damage was inflicted by German invasions in the late 3rd and early 5th centuries AD. Recovery and calm prosperity marked the intervening period, but the 5th century was a time of disaster in which Roman rule was only tenuously maintained in part of the country. When the line of western emperors ceased in 476, the Visigoths were the only recognizable authority in Spain; the subsequent restoration of imperial rule to the southern part of the country by Justinian is poorly documented.

Characteristic monuments of Spain are the inevitable city walls, which as in Gaul often enclose only a small part of the ancient cities. Examples of those may be seen at Barcelona, Leon and Conimbriga; the exceptionally well-preserved walls of Lugo in Galicia, on the other hand, enclose the whole of the small Classical town. City life, though reduced, still flourished in several cases. At Merida, the capital of Lusitania, Constantine and his sons restored the theater and circus, and a large private house of the usual peristyle type was converted into a Christian church. Belo, in Andalusia, shows activity of a very different kind; in addition to poorly built houses and shops, extensive remains of a factory for *garum* have survived. The late antique cookbook, attributed to the gourmet Apicius, shows how *garum*, a kind of sauce made from fish entrails and brine, was used in virtually every dish.

Like Gaul, Spain had its share of villas, most of them built or expanded in the 4th century, and many used well into the 5th when they continued as centers of Roman culture and resistance against the barbarians. One of particular interest has been excavated at Centcelles near Tarragona, where the main domed building was transformed into a mausoleum, perhaps for Constans, the son of Constantine. The dome contains the finest mosaics of their kind in Spain, featuring Cupids, Biblical scenes, and an elaborate hunt, perhaps a Christian allegory.

North Africa. In North Africa the Latin-speaking provinces stretched from Morocco to Libya. The richest part (modern Algeria and Tunisia) consisted of a coastal zone, which stretched some 90 miles inland and prospered from wheat, vines and stock raising, and the interior which subsisted from its vast olive production, supported by the irrigation works which the Romans had extended far towards the desert. To the east, the habitable zone of Tripolitania and Cyrenaica was much shallower, but still prosperous. Most of this vast area escaped the troubles of the 3rd century to flourish through the period.

The revolt against Maximinus in 238 AD brought bloody suppression, and tribal unrest caused the loss of the westernmost province by the time of Diocletian, but the greatest threats were internal: corruption, revolt and religious dissension. The case of Romanus and the city of Leptis has already been noted. Such an administration provoked serious revolts which did extensive damage, but far more disruptive was the wave of sectarian violence which convulsed the province for most of the 4th century. The Donatists, opposing forgiveness for their weaker brethren who had lapsed from the faith under persecution, fought bitterly against their Catholic rivals. Bands of poor peasants and migrant workers, inspired by the righteous doctrine of the heretics, formed armed bands called Circumcellions and attacked Catholic villas and churches until they and their Church were ruthlessly suppressed by the government after 411.

By that time, Roman rule was almost at an end. The

Above: the work of Justinian. Mosaic of 539 from Olbia in Cyrenaica showing the "New City, Theodorias"; the place had been rebuilt and named for the Empress Theodora. Part of the mosaic of 50 panels made by Alexandrian artisans.

Opposite: Roman Africa. The triumphal arch at Ammaedara encased in a small fortification wall.

whole nation of the Vandals, numbering some 80,000 people, crossed into Africa in 429 after ravaging Gaul and Spain. Within 10 years the province was in their hands, and in 455 Tripolitania fell to them. The occupied lands fell rapidly into decay and stagnated until the troops of Justinian swiftly restored imperial rule in 533, but at enormous cost to the province. The easy conquest was succeeded by revolts and civil war, but order was finally established, to last almost a century until the Arabs began to attack. Cyrene fell to them in 643, and the rest was raided for half a century before Carthage was finally taken in 698. In this period, Africa was vastly changed from what it had been in late antiquity; a society of cities, small towns and villas had been replaced by one in which crowded forts maintained a precarious defense for the countryside.

Africa contained one large city – Carthage, only partially known because of successive occupation – and innumerable small towns, many of which show considerable prosperity, beginning with reconstruction and growth under Diocletian and lasting through the 4th century. This is especially evident from church construction: at Timgad, for example, 17 churches were built, and whole Christian quarters at Jemila and Hippo; while Tebessa is famous for a great monastic complex of the mid-4th century. The fate of the cities is typical of the province: Timgad, once a large town, was deserted during the Vandal period, and then became the site of a Byzantine fort, of only 90 by 60 meters; at Tebessa the inner city was heavily fortified and the monastery, left outside the new walls, was provided with its own defenses.

More conspicuous urban remains survive in Tripolitania and Cyrenaica. Leptis Magna was thriving in the early 4th century when new constructions adorned its center. The attack of the Austuriani, however, ruined the local economy by destroying the olive groves, and the city entered upon a decline which became precipitate under the Vandals. Under Justinian, new walls were built which included only the area near the harbor, but churches were constructed and the magnificent basilica of Severus (a native of Leptis) was converted into a church. Sabratha similarly suffered from the Austuriani and contracted to half its former size, but there was considerable rebuilding and construction of new and large basilican churches.

In Cyrenaica, Cyrene declined while its nearby port Apollonia vigorously survived. Cyrene was ruined by an earthquake in 365 AD, then suffered the attacks of the Austuriani in 390 and later. The elegant public buildings and open spaces of the Classical city were gradually built over with small and shoddy constructions; this is particularly evident in the forum, the agora and the main streets. A few new structures, however, were of a higher standard, notably a private house in the center, a theater built over the marketplace, a bath erected on the ruins of a larger Classical one, and the cathedral church with its fine mosaics. During the decline provoked by the earthquake and the raids, the eastern part of the city was abandoned, leaving the cathedral separately fortified outside the walls. Apollonia, the capital of the province in the 6th century, saw no reduction but much new building. Several fine churches came to adorn the city and attest to its prosperity, as did the dominating palace of the local commandant, built in the time of Anastasius. This consisted of a group of rooms around a court, with a long audience hall, a chapel, a council chamber and quarters for the guard. Other cities suffered varying fates, some abandoned, others maintained, and even refounded as new cities.

Africa, the rich agricultural country and supplier of food for Rome, was famous for its great estates. The emperor was the largest owner, along with members of the Roman aristocracy, but tribal chiefs and local magnates also had substantial holdings. The southern frontier was defended by forts, in Tripolitania and Cyrenaica relatively closer to the sea. In those provinces, where security was less well established, individual farmhouses were heavily walled and virtually indistinguishable from forts.

Sicily. Sicily seems to have slumbered in obscurity until it was attacked, then conquered (in 468) by the Vandals, who soon sold it to the Goths. They in turn yielded easily to Belisarius in 535, and the island survived to become an important Byzantine province. In the time of Pope Gregory the Great (590–604) it was a peaceful and prosperous land. It was not, however, a place where urban life flourished. Although Syracuse, Palermo, Catania and a few other towns prospered – the population of some is suggested by their vast catacombs – the rest lapsed into obscurity or abandonment. Most of the country was owned by the emperor, the Church and the Roman senate. These men and their representatives built lavish villas, including one of the most spectacular in the empire, that of Piazza Armerina.

The end of Roman Italy. Invasion and civil war brought crisis and decline to Italy in the 3rd century as various pretenders marched in to seize supreme power, while German tribes crossed the Alps and the plague took its toll. The emperors, concentrating on the needs of defense, stayed closer to the frontier than Rome; under Maximian, Milan became the capital of the west, a role it maintained for almost a century. Cities were mostly in decline, the smaller ones having been replaced by villas. Small farms survived in most parts of the country, but brigandage was endemic and agriculture was far from prosperous. After an age of recovery, peace and stagnation, disaster struck Italy in the early 5th century, when the Goths overwhelmed it in a series of invasions which culminated in the sack of Rome by Alaric in 410 AD. In the meantime, the capital had moved to Ravenna, protected by miles of marshes. The attacks of Attila, who approached Rome in 452, and Gaiseric, the Vandal king who captured it in 455, were no less devastating. Roman Italy did not long survive; when the Goth Odoacer called his people in to settle and deposed the last puppet emperor in 476, the mother country, like the other western provinces, had fallen to the barbarians. Odoacer in turn yielded after a bitter struggle to Theodoric (489–526) whose wise administration did what it could to restore the battered country. But a decade after his death the troops of Belisarius brought imperial rule and a disastrous struggle which ruined whatever was left of the Italian economy. Hardly was Italy restored to the empire when it had to face a new and more successful invader, the Lombards, who came to control most of it for more than two centuries.

The monuments of the two capitals, Rome and Ravenna, far outshine anything else in the Western Empire. Nevertheless, there are other important remains in Italy: the churches of Aquileia, Grado and especially Milan should be mentioned, along with the villa at Desenzano on Lake Garda, and the elegant private houses of Ostia; most of those date from the 4th century.

Politically, Rome was in decline from the mid-3rd century, a process accelerated by the foundation of Constantinople. It remained, however, the seat of the senate, whose fabulously wealthy members owned vast tracts in the west and rose to the highest positions in the administration; moreover, the imperial city became the capital of the Church, which prospered from rich endowments as the empire collapsed around it.

Monuments of Rome and Ravenna. Even in eclipse, Rome was adorned with enormous and opulent monuments worthy of the capital of the world. The earliest of the period and clearest witness to its troubles is the great wall of Aurelian. Diocletian was responsible for the senate house in the Roman Forum, a building typical of the age with its simple and unified interior rendered bright with polychrome marbles, and for the greatest of the imperial baths, named after him. Maxentius began a vast basilica in the Forum, and completed a temple in memory of his son Romulus there, as well as a villa on the Appian Way with a well-preserved circus and a mausoleum in the style of the Pantheon. He was defeated and succeeded by Constantine, who completed the basilica, providing it with a colossal statue of himself, and commemorated his victory at the Milvian bridge with his famous arch near the Colosseum. The round mausoleum for his daughter Constantia with its fine decorative mosaics survives as the church of S. Costanza; another round building, the so-called temple of Minerva Medica, actually a pavilion, is probably contemporary. All this architecture is characterized by simple exteriors of brick, lavish and brightly decorated interiors, and grandiose and novel conceptions.

Great secular buildings ceased to be built after the time

The Baths of Diocletian in Rome. The interior of Michelangelo's church of S. Maria degli Angeli, built into the *tepidarium*, gives an idea of the scale and decor of the baths.

of Constantine, but the variety of ecclesiastical architecture shows that the power and wealth of the Church continued and grew. Its first imperial patrons, Constantine and Helen, were responsible for the only two large churches within the walls, the basilicas of the Lateran and of S. Croce in Gerusalemme. The others were built outside the walls, partly because of the strength of the pagan aristocracy, but also in conformity with the Christian custom of celebrating the memory of saints and martyrs with meetings and banquets. As the congregation grew, simple enclosures in the graveyards (all outside the city) were expanded into permanent meeting halls; of those, the churches of S. Lorenzo fuori le Mura, S. Agnese and S. Sebastiano were Constantinian.

The situation changed by the late 4th century with a period of church construction within the walls. The most interesting is perhaps S. Clemente where a basilica of about 390 was built over an older private house which contained a chapel to the god Mithra; similarly SS. Giovanni e Paolo covers a house with Christian chapels. These reveal the origin of the city churches as meeting-places in the houses of the faithful, where gatherings could be held without attracting undue attention. Of the same period, the great churches of S. Paolo, S. Maria Maggiore,

Above: the mausoleum of Galla Placidia (440 AD) in Ravenna. The interior is decorated with outstanding mosaics. Much of Roman Ravenna survives to illustrate the fashions of late antique architecture.

Below: Piranesi's engraving of the Basilica of Maxentius and Constantine. The last great monument of the Roman Forum, begun in 306 and finished after 313, overwhelms the viewer with its arches.

S. Stefano Rotondo and S. Sabina, the latter with a remarkable resemblance to the Basilica of Trier, show the characteristics of late antique church architecture, as do some dozen smaller churches. Thereafter, with the decline of Italy, construction abated; the 6th century produced S. Maria Antiqua and SS. Cosma e Damiano on the Forum, while S. Lorenzo and S. Agnese were completely rebuilt after Justinian. Most of the late antique churches are finely decorated with marble, fresco or mosaics, some extremely well preserved.

The Christians of Rome are famous as well for their underground monuments in the catacombs; Christian tombs in these vast complexes abound from the earliest days of the faith until the 5th century when the land outside the walls became too unsafe, even for burials. The tombs usually consist of niches in the underground corridors, or in small rooms off them; they are frequently adorned with shrines and chapels. Similar examples may be seen in Naples.

Honorius and his successors worked splendidly to make the port town of Ravenna worthy of a capital, and a remarkable proportion of their work survives to illustrate the fashions of late antique architecture. To the time of Honorius, his sister Galla Placidia and her son Valentinian III belong the baptistery of the orthodox, a simple octagonal structure, the basilica of S. Giovanni Evangelista and the mausoleum of Galla Placidia, the last two

Opposite: the famous mosaic of paradise in the apse of S. Apollinare in Classe, Ravenna.

Below: the Arch of Constantine in Rome. The arch illustrates an age which unabashedly plundered the useless treasures of its glorious past to decorate its own work.

decorated with outstanding mosaics. Theodoric continued the tradition and taste for color in the baptistery of the Arians (his Teutonic followers were heretics), the church of S. Apollinare Nuovo and his own massive mausoleum. Justinian typically left an even more magnificent monument in his church of S. Vitale, a complex structure on an octagonal plan which gives a similar impression to St Sophia. The contemporary basilica of S. Apollinare in Classe, with its famous mosaic of paradise, is also impressive. In general, the mosaics of Ravenna are the finest surviving examples in the empire.

The Balkans. Across the Adriatic lay Dalmatia, a narrow coast with cities which served as markets for the mountainous interior. Protected by its mountain barrier, the coast was spared invasion until 395 AD, when the Visigoths caused considerable damage. In 454 the general Marcellinus made the province virtually independent, but in 480 it fell to the Goths, to be reconquered by Justinian in 536. Thereafter, decline was rapid as Slavs and Avars overran the interior, then the coast; Salona, the largest city, was destroyed in 612, and only a few towns and islands remained to the empire.

Salona prospered through the period; even the refortification of Justinian includes virtually the whole ancient city. It is especially famous for the remains of its churches, within and without the walls, which have made it a center for the study of early Christian architecture. Nearby was the great palace of Diocletian. Remains are fewer in the less populated interior, but the fortified villa of Mogorilo and the curative spa of Aquae S . . . (the rest of the name is unknown), both near Sarajevo, are important monuments.

The lands of the long and exposed Danube frontier suffered the worst damage and are the poorest in remains in the empire. The western part, Pannonia (parts of Austria, Hungary and Yugoslavia), was overrun by the Germans in the 250s and 270s, a time when it was also the scene of revolt and civil war. Diocletian and his successors, using Sirmium as a base, restored peace, and Constantius II was even able to advance against the tribes in the Hungarian plain. In the reign of Valentinian, however, invasions began again; the worst attacks came in 380 and 395, the latter so severe that most settlements were destroyed, Roman control effectively brought to an end, and the land occupied by barbarians. Roman rule lingered on until the arrival of the Ostrogoths in 406; further south, Sirmium was Roman until its conquest by Attila in 442.

The fate of Aquincum (Budapest) illustrates that of the region. Buildings destroyed in the 3rd century were not rebuilt, hypocausts were replaced by hearths, drains no longer functioned. The population withdrew into the legionary fortress, while the civilian settlement which had extended outside was abandoned to become a graveyard. The ruins of Brigetio and Carnuntum tell a similar story, though the latter is distinguished by a triumphal arch to commemorate the victories of Constantius II.

Within the frontier, life could still prosper. Justinian wished to adorn his birthplace, a village south of Nish; its remains, at Caricin Grad, illustrate his success. A substantial town, with an acropolis, a lower settlement and large churches, was built in one great project. Further south, in Macedonia, the ruins of Stobi are those of a prosperous town. Churches, a synagogue, baths, a palace and comfortable town houses line the two main streets; all were built or restored in the 4th and 5th centuries, when Stobi was the provincial capital. After the Ostrogothic attack of 479, however, signs of decline are evident as the town became crowded with refugees from the countryside.

The eastern Balkans, devastated by barbarians and the plague, and the site of two of the worst disasters in Roman history – the defeat and death of Decius in 251 and Valens in 378 – have preserved relatively few remains. The troubles of the 3rd century were so serious that the province north of the Danube, Dacia, had to be abandoned. Diocletian and Constantine restored order, which was interrupted by the Visigoths in 379 and Attila in 441–42 and 447. The Huns so devastated the provinces that restoration only took place under Justinian, but not long afterwards Slavs and Avars began to invade and most of the region was soon lost.

The bridgeheads of Drobeta and Sucidava on the north bank of the Danube illustrate Roman determination to guard the vital frontier. In both cases the towns were given up when Dacia was evacuated, but forts built by Constantine lasted until destroyed by Attila. Raised from their ruins by Justinian, they both fell to the Avars at the end of the 6th century. Further east, near the estuary of the Danube, Troesmis and Dinogetia contain extensive remains which reveal the nature of such small fortified towns with their commandant's headquarters, barracks, houses and churches.

The cities of the Black Sea, better protected than those of the interior, experienced a greater prosperity evidenced by such remains as the huge mosaic at Tomi, the churches, houses and fortifications of Histria, and the basilica of Mesembria, mostly monuments of the 4th and 6th centuries. Remains in the interior are sparser. Nicopolis on the Istrus, rebuilt by Constantine and Justinian, has a bath of the 4th century, and somewhat later fortifications survive at Philippopolis. The most substantial remains, of two brick churches, stand at Serdica (Sofia), a residence of Constantine and center of refugees from Dacia. Although destroyed by Attila, it rose from its ruins and remained in imperial hands until the Middle Ages.

Greece. Greece was not saved by its distance from the ravaged frontier. In 267 AD the Goths and Heruli, after destroying Athens and Corinth, penetrated into the Peloponnese, and Alaric in 395 spread destruction over the whole country. Attila reached Thermopylae, the Vandals ravaged the west coast. The greatest troubles, however,

Above: the massive walls of Thessalonica. Begun in the 4th century, they kept the city free from capture.

Top: the church of St George in Sofia. Originally part of a Roman bath, this building of typical brick construction was converted into a church in the 5th century.

Opposite: Troesmis on the Danube. This Justinianic military foundation shows a highly organized plan, with the northern part dominated by the governor and the bishop, the southern by the army. After MacKendrick.

came in the 6th century: Huns in 540, the plague two years later, then the constant invasions of the Avars and Slavs who overran the whole country, destroyed most of what remained of city life and caused widespread depopulation in the country.

The greatest city in Greece was Thessalonica, whose massive walls kept it free from capture, and whose role as administrative center caused it to be decorated with impressive monuments. Galerius made the city his residence, and had an enormous palace built there; much later it became the capital of the prefecture of Illyricum (the European provinces controlled by Constantinople)

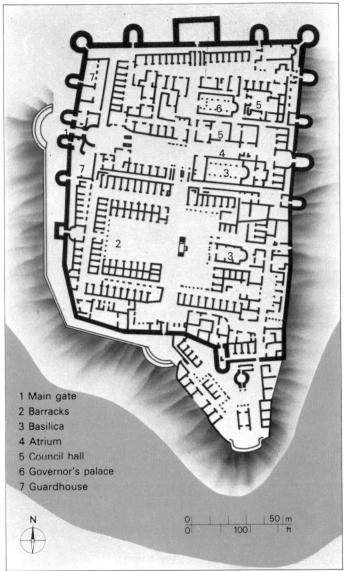

1 Main gate
2 Barracks
3 Basilica
4 Atrium
5 Council hall
6 Governor's palace
7 Guardhouse

N

0   50 | m
0   100 | | ft

when Attila took Sirmium. The work of Galerius consisted of a complex of buildings forming a palace which stretched from the sea almost half a mile into the city. Of this, a rotunda, a triumphal arch and an octagonal building, which may have been a throne room, are preserved; next to the octagon was the entrance to the hippodrome, an integral part of the complex.

As the capital of the prefecture, Thessalonica saw one of the greatest building programs of the empire. Evidence for this sudden activity comes from stamps used on the bricks, which show that many buildings were contemporary. These included a new palace in the center of the city, new fortification walls, the conversion of the rotunda into a church, and the construction of at least three churches, that of St David, a small domed structure, and the two imposing basilicas of the Acheiropoetos and of St Demetrius.

Elsewhere in Greece, basilican churches illustrate the growth of Christianity and the relative wealth of the province in the 4th and 5th centuries. Philippi in Mac-

edonia is the site of several important churches, as is Nea Anchialos in Thessaly and Nicopolis in Epirus. Lechaion, the port of Corinth, contains the remains of one of the largest churches of the age, a 6th-century basilica over 300 feet long, so huge that there is considerable doubt whether it was ever finished.

The history of Athens may be taken to illustrate the fate of many cities in Greece. Excavations in the agora, the ancient marketplace and civic center, show the violence of the attack of the Heruli in 267; the buildings were burned, and a new wall was built of their ruins to include only a small part of the ancient city; much of the agora, left outside, was deserted for a century. In the early 5th century recovery came when a complex of buildings with baths, a gymnasium and pagan decor was erected; it has been identified as the philosophical school which made the city famous in late antiquity and flourished until closed by Justinian in 529. Other rebuildings within the walls probably represent a concentration of population from the countryside. The appearance of Athena and Achilles, together with a substantial bribe, kept Alaric and his Goths away from Athens, but there was much to fear from other invaders. Finally, in the 580s, the Slavs so destroyed the city that it was inhabited only by squatters for a long time.

The city of Constantinople. The last city in the European half of the empire was the greatest and most important, Constantinople, the New Rome. According to the legend, Constantine, having resolved to found a new capital, settled on Troy, and had actually begun construction when a vision inspired him to move to Byzantium, strategically located at the gateway between Europe and Asia, the Mediterranean and the Black Sea. The site he chose was well defended by nature, with water on three sides, and by the great walls on the landward side. Its defenses were one of the major factors in ensuring continuity of imperial rule in the east.

The center of Constantine's city was a square called the Augusteum on which the greatest monuments of the city faced: the Senate House, the Great Palace, the Hippodrome and a large public bath. Immediately to the west stood the golden milestone, from which distances all over the empire were measured. From there, the main boulevard led westward, lined with shops and bazaars, through a series of forums, each the center of a district and site of a large market; the first was the Forum of Constantine, which contained a column with a statue of the founder of the city, then the Forum of Theodosius, decorated with a huge and remarkably ugly arch, then the Amastrianum, the Forum of the Ox, and the Forum of Arcadius with a column 140 feet high bearing a statue of that emperor. Finally, after about four miles, the street reached the mighty walls of the city and the Golden Gate, a triumphal arch of Theodosius adorned with a verse inscription associating the Golden Gate with the golden age which the emperor brought. The walls here are those built by

Theodosius II in 443; the city of Constantine had been considerably smaller, but such a multitude flocked to the new capital that it had to expand westward. This western part, however, was never so densely inhabited as the rest of the city, and provided space for the open cisterns – some 500 feet square and 30 feet deep – built in the 5th century and still visible.

No expense was spared in building and adorning the new capital, and cities throughout the empire were ransacked for their works of art. During the first part of its existence, Constantinople was rarely the imperial residence; Constantius and Valens preferred Antioch. Only with Theodosius did the emperors finally settle in Constantinople, and after his time they rarely left it.

Of the work of Constantine, nothing has survived but the column which bore his statue. The basic work of construction was only completed under Constantius, and most of the late antique remains have been destroyed in subsequent rebuildings, for the city has never ceased to be important and densely inhabited. Little remains from the 4th century, but its most notable monument is one of the most important in the city, the Hippodrome, where the chariot races which attracted such a fanatical following were held. At the same time, the Hippodrome was a center of political life for the population, for only here could they reach the ears of the autocratic government by acclamation or riot. The *spina* of the Hippodrome was adorned with an Egyptian obelisk, the column of three serpents from Delphi which the Greeks had set up to commemorate their victory at Plataea, statues to successful charioteers and innumerable masterpieces of Classical art. Some of these are still visible in a square which preserves the shape of the Hippodrome, whose high retaining wall also partially survives. The same period saw the construction of the aqueduct of Valens, still standing over the center of the city: it provided the water supply which was stored in vast underground or open cisterns.

The 5th century produced the city walls, two palaces and two churches – St John of Studium, a famous monastery near the walls, and St Mary of the Coppersmith's Quarter, near St Sophia. One of the palaces was the Great Palace of the emperors of which a few rooms have been discovered east of the Hippodrome; they are decorated with a floor mosaic with naturalistic scenes of people, plants and animals. The other palace, with a complex arrangement of circular, hexagonal and octagonal rooms, stood on the other side of the Hippodrome.

The greatest monuments by far are those of the age of Justinian, especially three churches. The earliest, Sts Sergius and Bacchus near the sea walls, is built on an elegant and unusual plan consisting of a domed octagon within a square; the building has galleries and a long inscription below them praising the works of the Empress Theodora. Somewhat later is the huge domed basilica of St Irene, burned in the Nika revolt, and rebuilt by Justinian. These and all the other remains, however, pale

An underground cistern of Justinian engraved by Thomas Allom in 1840 and colored by Laura Lushington. This cavernous structure under the center of Constantinople stored water for the Great Palace and contained 336 Corinthian columns 25 feet high.

before the magnificence of the *chef d'oeuvre* of late antiquity, the church of St Sophia.

St Sophia. When the original church, founded by Constantius II, was destroyed in the Nika revolt, Justinian resolved to replace it with a far greater building. Of all his achievements, this, along with the codification of the Roman law, was the most successful and enduring. The empire was pillaged for materials and decorations, and 10,000 men worked on the building under the watchful eye of the emperor who visited the site almost daily. In five years the audacious and grandiose structure was completed, and Justinian, entering it on the day of its dedication, 27 December 537, could proudly (and perhaps justly) exclaim "I have conquered thee, O Solomon."

The uniqueness of the church lies in its size and architectural conception. Within a rectangle of 70 × 76 meters, four huge pillars form a square 30 meters on a side. They support arches which begin to spring 20 meters from the ground and in turn provide pendentives to hold up the vast dome, 30 meters in diameter, which rises 52 meters above the floor. Outside this central core, other piers, walls and columns provide side aisles and support internal arcades and the exterior structure of the church. The interior gives an impression of loftiness and elegant lightness. The lower parts were covered with a wealth of multicolored marble which contrasted with the gray marble paving slabs; the capitals and arcades above them were decorated with a delicate filigree of cut marble, and the highest reaches were covered with mosaics. All around hung gold and silver lamps; 20 tons of silver alone were employed in the decorations. As the eye of the beholder rose upward towards the dome, the light, passing through windows of colored glass, gradually became brighter, but always remained subdued.

In accordance with the canons of late antiquity, the exterior is relatively plain, in great contrast to Classical architecture, where the focus was on the outside. But even the exterior of St Sophia is impressive with its square

The monument of Porphyrius. A stele erected to honor the greatest charioteer of his day, the 6th-century popular hero Porphyrius, in the Hippodrome of Constantinople, where he won his many victories. Archaeological Museum, Istanbul.

The emperor at the Hippodrome. Theodosius presiding at the games from the imperial loge, a suite of rooms connected directly with the Great Palace. He holds a wreath for the winning charioteer; below, spectators, dancers and an orchestra.

buttresses and half-domes leading up to the main dome which towers over the skyline of the city, symbol of the triumphant glory of God and of Justinian. The former may, as the Byzantines believed, have protected the city against all its foes; the megalomania of the latter, which led to this stunning monument, produced also the reconquest of the west, the misgovernment and oppression of the rest to finance his vast schemes, and perhaps the ultimate collapse of the empire.

The Eastern Empire. The narrative of the provinces so far considered has perforce been concerned with wars, invasions, devastations and loss; the western provinces, with few exceptions, were troubled throughout late antiquity. By the end of the 5th century all of them had been lost to Roman rule, and only a few were regained by Justinian, whose work, achieved at terrible cost, soon collapsed. It is thus a striking contrast to turn to the eastern half of the empire, where most of the age was spent in comfortable and somnolent prosperity. Since the provinces from the Bosphorus to Egypt were Roman until the 7th century and suffered little disturbance after the 3rd, the history of all of them may be treated summarily together.

The crisis of the 3rd century did not spare the eastern provinces. The new and aggressive Sasanian dynasty in Persia inflicted the greatest humiliation the Romans had yet experienced in 260, when the Emperor Valerian was taken captive. At the same time, Gothic raids descended on Asia Minor. During the series of revolts and civil wars which followed, Zenobia of Palmyra was able to bring most of the east under her sway. Aurelian defeated her and began to restore order, a process completed by Diocletian and Constantine, whose work, combined with the heavy fortifications of the frontier, secured peace for three centuries. Subsequent disturbances were local.

On the frontier, war was endemic. Carus and Julian penetrated as far as the Persian capital, but with little effect. Galerius won major victories on the frontier and Constantius II had to fight long campaigns there. More serious trouble came during the reign of Justinian when the Persian King Chosroes in 540 destroyed Antioch, the greatest city of the east. Roman supremacy was finally secured by Maurice, who added new territory to the empire after a long struggle, but unparalleled disaster struck the Romans after his death. Chosroes II invaded and within 15 years had conquered all the eastern provinces. Although his work was undone in a decade, the damage which his forces inflicted was permanent. Asia Minor and Syria were in ruins; so many cities had been destroyed that

the Classical urban culture was at an end. Not long after Heraclius recovered the remnants of his empire, a new foe appeared and everything south of the Taurus was lost forever to the Arabs.

Compared with the west, the eastern provinces were old and highly developed. Except for Egypt, they were covered with a network of cities and innumerable villages. Since they flourished in the three centuries of late antiquity, the eastern provinces preserve far richer remains than the west. The urban culture may be best appreciated in Asia Minor, and village life in Syria; the Holy Land and Egypt are famous for their churches and monasteries. Such is the wealth of remains that only the most important can be considered here.

Urban culture in Asia Minor. The fertile coastal region of Asia Minor had always been one of the richest and most densely populated of the empire, renowned for its vast number of flourishing cities. In late antiquity, these cities came to take on a different appearance from the Classical, as churches and fortifications were built, temples aban-

Opposite: the nave of St Sophia, completed in 537. According to the contemporary Procopius, the columns seemed to perform a choral dance, the piers were like mountain peaks and the dome seemed suspended from Heaven.

Right: the walls of Nicaea. *Above,* as they appear on a coin of the usurper Quietus (260–61), when they were under construction (British Museum); *below,* one of the towers as now preserved.

doned and used as quarries, and fashions changed so that, for example, open markets tended to be replaced by bazaars lining the streets.

Besides Ephesus (which is described elsewhere), late antique cities may be seen at Sardis, Miletus, Aphrodisias and Hierapolis in the west of Asia Minor, and Side on the south coast; numerous others contain substantial buildings of the period. At Nicaea, for example, the fortifications of the late 3rd century are well preserved. Sardis presents a whole quarter built in the period, with shops along colonnaded streets, a large basilica, and a chapel and urban villas; in addition, a Roman gymnasium complex which had come to include a large synagogue was remodeled in the 5th century and maintained until the Persians destroyed the city in 616. Miletus saw considerable activity under the Tetrarchy, when its stadium and theater were rebuilt, and in the 6th century when its cathedral church with splendid mosaics was erected and a large Roman gymnasium remodeled. Outside the city the famous temple of Apollo at Didyma had a curious history. In the late 3rd century, under the threat of Gothic attack, it was fortified, and defended by troops who were miraculously kept alive by a spring of water which the god provided. After the triumph of Christianity, the temple was converted into a church which eventually became the center of a settlement.

Aphrodisias, as it now appears, is essentially as it was in the 6th century when it was provincial capital, with its marble forums and squares and public buildings, its elaborate churches (the greatest converted from the temple of Aphrodite), and its remarkably well-preserved stadium, incorporated as a bastion into the city wall. At Hierapolis the most imposing monuments are the churches – five large basilicas, and an elaborate octagonal martyrium outside the walls overlooking the city. Side, on the south coast, reflects a different historical development. In the 4th century, probably as a result of Isaurian attacks, a new wall was built which only enclosed half the city; subsequently expansion took place and the large area within the old Hellenistic walls came again to be occupied. The city is notable for its broad colonnaded streets, large churches and 5th-century baths.

On a smaller scale than these cities, which bear comparison with those of the Classical period, there are important remains of small towns, especially in the south. Among these is Kanlidivane in Cilicia, where several churches, numerous public buildings and small houses are extremely well preserved. The same region preserves many exceptionally fine floor mosaics which adorned local churches and houses.

Asia Minor was early a great center of Christianity and soon provided a fertile ground for monasticism. Some monks withdrew to remote areas, particularly mountains; others established themselves in or near cities. The great age of monasticism in Asia Minor came in the Byzantine period, but the remains show that the movement was already important in late antiquity. Notable among them are Bin Bir Kilise ("the 1,001 churches") in the southern part of the central steppe, where dozens of small churches, mostly on the basilican plan, clustered together in the remoteness of a sacred mountain, and the elegant monastic complex of Alahan in the Taurus.

Southeast of Anatolia stretched the monotonous plains of Roman Mesopotamia, rich in wheat and valuable for their strategic location between Rome and Persia. The great battles between the two empires were fought here, and the country was consequently marked by heavily fortified cities, able to withstand long sieges. Imposing Roman fortifications are to be seen at Diyarbakir (Amida) and Dara on the frontier, with fragments in many other sites. The province was also noted as a center of monasticism, especially that part of it known as the Tur Abdin, an elevated plateau where a large number of important foundations still survive. The churches, built on a variety of plans in the 6th century and later, are distinguished by their fine, regularly cut masonry and stone decoration, and the complexes of monastic buildings around them.

Village life in Syria. The province of Syria is one of the richest in late antique remains. Because of their solid stone construction and long abandonment, many sites of small towns and villages have survived in a remarkable state of preservation. They give a detailed impression of the life of a countryside quite different from the Classical world which it adjoined, a countryside of peasants and prosperous small farmers, devoted to their unorthodox Church and its leaders, the local holy men.

Classical city life existed on a large scale in Syria, but has left few traces, as if time had removed a veneer of Hellenism to leave the rustic Syrian core visible. One of the greatest cities of the empire was in Syria – Antioch, the residence of emperors in the 4th century, the site of a great palace, a famous cathedral and numerous magnificent monumental buildings, all now vanished. The city flourished until its destruction in 540; a similar fate befell Aleppo and other places. The prosperity of the age, however, has left abundant traces in the great collection of mosaics discovered in Antioch and its environs, originally the decorations of the numerous villas of the urban rich.

The hills around Antioch and Aleppo have preserved a network of innumerable villages, mostly dating from the 4th to 6th centuries, a time of great prosperity in the countryside, which continued until the Persian invasions. The hilly country depended on the cultivation of the olive, a product which came into greater demand after the loss of the western provinces which had produced great quantities of it. The olive growers seem to have been small landowners for the most part; although there are remains of many villas, these are tiny establishments compared with the kind so far considered. The villages are of many different types, large and small, rich and poor, ranging from small clusters of poor houses to large agglomerations

The bazaar at Sardis. Part of a long row of small shops with an upper floor and glass windows, built in the 4th century.

with substantial dwellings, baths and other public buildings. All have two features in common; they contain a church, sometimes several, and are built of neatly cut stone. In general, the architecture is of a local, non-Classical kind; the buildings are square and blockish, simple on the interior with some exterior decoration. Plans of the buildings, especially of the churches, vary considerably within a common framework.

In this land of saints and villagers, some holy men attained exceptional fame. The most imposing monument of the country is probably that associated with the name of the famous pillar saint, Simeon, who lived for 30 years on top of a column 20 meters high on a mountain not far from Antioch. Recognized as a fabulous holy man and wonder worker in his own day, Simeon became the subject of a cult after his death, and attracted such throngs of pilgrims that a unique and grandiose series of buildings was erected around 470 to commemorate his memory and accommodate his worshipers. The buildings centered on an octagonal room built around the column of the saint; from it radiated four basilican halls, each 24 meters or more long, the longest, to the east, being the actual church building. Adjacent to this, and enclosed in the same wall, was a large monastery. The crowds who came to worship did not stay in the monastery, but in the neighboring town of Telanissos at the bottom of the hill, a place which had begun as an agricultural village but developed into a great resort full of large hotels.

St Simeon started a fashion of sitting on pillars, and the stylite saints who followed his example were prominent for centuries. One of them, also called Simeon, mortified his flesh in the region of Antioch. His column also came to provide a site for a monastic complex, imitating that of his great namesake, on a mountain southwest of the city.

The Syrians did not all live peacefully in such cities, villages or pillars. Many inhabited the frontier, where constant defense was a necessity against an enemy who might suddenly approach. One of the most famous cities

The walls of Dara. Built by Anastasius to defend the frontier, the town became one of the greatest Roman bulwarks against the Sasanians; the outside wall was added by Justinian.

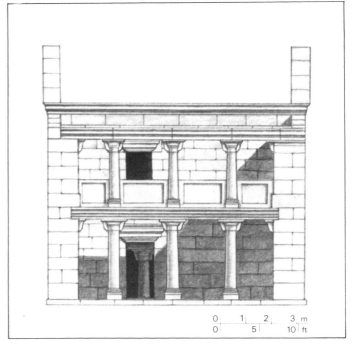

The facade of the café at Serjilla, a Syrian village of the 5th century. Reconstruction after Butler.

of the frontier, Dura-Europus, had been captured by the Persians in 256, and completely abandoned thereafter. It offers a complete picture of a Roman frontier town of the beginning of the period, one which contained both Jewish and Christian colonies; its church is the oldest known. Among other notable frontier posts are Resafah on the Euphrates, surrounded by a rectangular wall 500 × 300 meters, within which is preserved the monumental 6th-century basilica of the local saint, Sergius, and the complex of Qasr ibn Wardan in the desert northeast of Hama where a church, a palace and a barracks stand isolated on a rise, built in the time of Justinian in the style of buildings in the capital.

Arabia. The southern part of Syria and modern Jordan formed part of the Roman province of Arabia, where it is possible to appreciate both city and village life. Two caravan cities flourished in the period and contain extensive remains. The northern, and capital of the province, was Bosra, built on a Classical plan with two colonnaded streets intersecting at a triumphal arch; its ruins include a large domed cathedral and bishop's palace, as well as other churches.

Much more impressive are the remains of Gerasa, a Classical city extensively rebuilt in late antiquity, and one of the finest sites in the eastern provinces. The city was built on a regular plan with a long colonnaded street which ran through the center; its intersections with two other boulevards were marked by tetrapyla (four-sided arches). At the south tetrapylon a round plaza with shops was the work of the time of Diocletian. The greatest

building of the ancient city was the temple of Artemis approached from the east through an elaborate colonnaded courtyard. At the end of the reign of Justinian the courtyard was converted into a church, one of 13 so far discovered. The earliest of the churches was the 4th-century cathedral built next to the temple of Artemis over a temple of Dionysus, and approached by stairs from the main street; like most of the churches, it was built on the basilican plan, but was distinguished by a large courtyard in which the miracle of changing water into wine was annually enacted. Of the other churches, most were built in the reign of Justinian or later; the last is dated to 611, immediately before the Persian attack. The churches were decorated with fine mosaic floors, but are of generally mediocre construction. Contemporary with them are clear signs of change and deterioration in urban life: the elegant Roman forum was built over with small houses, and the precinct of the temple was occupied by huts and pottery kilns, showing that the apparent revival of the city under Justinian was of limited extent.

As in Syria, small towns and villages have survived in remarkable preservation. The site of Umm el-Jimal (its ancient name is not known), with its black basalt buildings rising from the desert, is an important example of the former. Behind its walls, it contains a governor's palace of the 4th century, a barracks building with tower, courtyard and chapel built in 412, and no fewer than 15 churches; the largest, the cathedral, a basilica like the others, was built

The monastery of St Simeon the Stylite, erected around 470 to commemorate him and accommodate his worshipers.

under Justinian, when the whole area was undergoing revival. In addition, there are numerous stone houses with courtyards, mostly of two stories, in irregular crooked streets. North of it, in the Hauran, there are extensive remains of villages of dark and crowded square stone buildings. The desert was also marked with fortresses to check the raids of the local tribes.

The Holy Land. Among the many boons which the conversion of Constantine brought the Christian Church, a vast influx of cash and the generous construction of palatial buildings must have been one of the most welcome. The generosity of the new convert was especially evident in the west at Rome, and in the east, not at Constantinople, but at Jerusalem and other sacred sites of the Holy Land. In 326 Helen, mother of Constantine, arrived in Jerusalem, then a desolate garrison town; she soon had the good fortune to discover the True Cross, and, together with her son, endowed numerous churches on the most sacred spots of the city, notable among them the churches of the Holy Sepulcher and of the Ascension and the basilica on the Mount of Olives. Other major church construction continued through the 4th century, but of all this virtually nothing has survived because of destruction and rebuilding. Jerusalem enjoyed two other periods of lavish imperial favor: in 444–60, when the Empress Eudocia took up residence in the city after a misunderstanding about her virtue with the emperor, and

during the reign of Justinian; each of these periods saw extensive construction and rebuilding of churches. Although very little has survived, a contemporary picture gives some idea of the appearance of the city.

The Holy Land by the 4th century became a famous center of pilgrimage and naturally prospered from the revenues which such activity brought. Pilgrimage and imperial munificence were not confined to Jerusalem. A great basilica was built at the spot where Christ was born in Bethlehem – the Church of the Nativity, constructed by Constantine and rebuilt by Justinian, in which state it has survived. Nor was the Old Testament neglected; one of Justinian's most impressive foundations was the monastery of St Catherine on Mount Sinai where mosaics and icons of the time have been religiously preserved. These have great importance in the history of art because of the wholesale destruction of religious pictures by the iconoclastic emperors in the lands under their control. The piety of late antiquity was displayed on another site associated with Moses, Mount Nebo, where he viewed the Promised Land and died. A basilica was expanded in the late 6th century into the surviving monastic complex; the church contains mosaic floors, now badly damaged, but the monastery is reasonably well preserved. A finer and more elaborate mosaic of the same period may be seen two miles to the south in the church of Sts Lot and Procopius.

Christians did not monopolize the Holy Land, but shared it with the Jews, whose activity is visible in the form of numerous synagogues put up in late antiquity. In plan these often resemble churches in that they are basilical and often have an apse, but, unlike the churches of the

The palace and church of Qasr ibn Wardan in the desert northeast of Hama, built in the time of Justinian.

region, they are not oriented toward the east, but to Jerusalem. Many of them are decorated with fine mosaics, some of which, contrary to expectation, show representational scenes with human figures, usually stories from the Old Testament. Other synagogues, the fruit of the diaspora, are to be found in many parts of the empire.

Egypt. Egypt was always unique in the Classical Mediterranean world, a country almost entirely without cities, a narrow strip of incredibly fertile land surrounded by limitless stretches of uninhabitable desert. One city was an exception, the great metropolis of Alexandria, with which only Antioch and Constantinople in the east could compare. Its numerous and sophisticated citizens felt a disdain for the upstart new capital and were fanatically loyal to their bishops who bitterly contested the claims of Constantinople for ecclesiastical supremacy. Alexandria had been laid out by the Ptolemies according to the most modern and elegant plans, and had never ceased to flourish and be beautified by each succeeding age. Late antiquity contributed its share of buildings, as it destroyed the old ones, most notably the famous temple of Sarapis, but decline and decay subsequently have reduced the work of ages to almost total oblivion. Other cities, hardly more than straggling towns or fortresses containing a few Greeks in a sea of Egyptians, have left somewhat more trace, but Egypt, because of the perishable materials used and the constant dense inhabitation of the country, is poor in late antique remains.

Babylon, at the head of the Delta, was one of the most strategic places in the province; its capture allowed the Arabs to overrun the rest freely. The site was defended by a powerful fortress with high round towers, still preserved in the old section of Cairo; it was probably built in the time of Arcadius. In Upper Egypt habitations of the period were excavated at Hermopolis Major, where they were built over and among the temples ruined by the Christians. The houses were small affairs of two stories and a cellar, with large windows, built of sun-dried brick on foundations of unfinished stones. At another site, the island of Philae, the local temple was not destroyed, but advantage of its great bulk was taken to convert it into a church; numerous graffiti, inscriptions and crosses carved on its wall, as well as structural alterations, witness the change. Even when buildings were not converted, it was customary to carve crosses on them to protect against the devils who were believed to dwell in the fabric of pagan structures.

Late antique Egypt was famous as the home of two quite different classes of people: rich landlords, and monks. Like the metropolis, the works of the former have vanished almost completely. More enduring have been the achievements and memory of the monks, for Egypt was the home of monasticism, which began in the dark days of the mid-3rd century when St Anthony took up his residence in the desert, far from human habitation. His

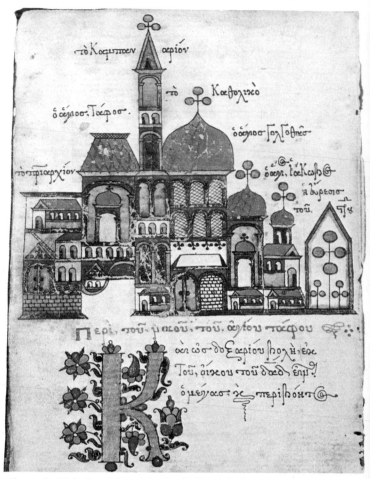

Above: the Holy Sepulcher and other buildings in Jerusalem as portrayed in the 17th-century Athos manuscript, Gregoriou 139.
Opposite above: a Jewish mosaic from the synagogue of Ma'on at Nirim. This mosaic of the late 5th century shows the seven-branched candlestick, symbolic of Judaism. Israel Museum, Jerusalem.
Opposite below: the monastery of St Catherine on Mount Sinai, one of Justinian's most impressive foundations.

example became overwhelmingly popular, and by the end of the century St Pachomius had established a form of organization on which monastic life came to be based. Since the monasteries were built on land that was useless for any other purpose, their sites have not been disturbed by dense habitation, but the continuing tradition of monasticism in the Coptic Church has meant that many of the original buildings have long since been remodeled beyond recognition. In addition to the communities, there were vast numbers of cells of individual monks and hermits, temporary shelters which have vanished.

Built on the desert, where any kind of threat might appear, the Egyptian monasteries were fortified and resemble desert castles with towns inside them. Two of the best examples from the period are the White and Red Monasteries near Sohag in Upper Egypt. A heavy fortification surrounds the monastic buildings which, in addition to churches, might include residences for the monks, hotels for pilgrims, courtyards, gardens and even baths. The White Monastery has an elaborate basilican

church with a trefoil apse; the Red Monastery is similar. Both are decorated in the local rigid and angular style; the White Monastery is of the 5th century, the Red of the 6th.

Patterns of settlement. This survey of the late antique monuments reflects both the universal culture of the age, and the diversity which marked it. Every region contained cities, villages, villas and fortresses, but their relative importance varied tremendously according to local historical developments and needs. In the east, where Classical civilization had originated and first flourished, city life was well established, and each district had a substantial metropolis or several large centers, while western Europe, where urban culture suffered a great blow in the 3rd century, contained only a few large cities in lands where villas and decentralization predominated. Everywhere, east and west, villages were scattered over the countryside because of the predominance of agriculture. Other regions showed different patterns of settlement: in Africa there were innumerable small cities dividing the rich grain-producing lands, while in Egypt,

which had an even greater production, the population lived almost exclusively in villages, except for the flourishing Greeks of Alexandria. In all parts of the empire, however, society and government were based on the cities.

Similarly, the same kind of buildings were built everywhere. A late antique city normally contained a full complement of public buildings – baths, theaters, senate houses, marketplaces, aqueducts etc. – which offered the inhabitants the range of free services that they had enjoyed under the early empire; but major changes took place. After the troubles of the 3rd century most cities were fortified, as they were to remain until modern times. With the triumph of Christianity they also came to take on a Christian appearance as temples were abandoned or destroyed and the ubiquitous basilican churches were erected everywhere in a style which remained remarkably unchanged until the time of Justinian. A common architecture and decoration also prevailed. Monumental buildings tended to reflect the ideas of the age by overawing the beholder with their stark simplicity, and by focusing his attention on a central point. They were almost universally covered with a bright carpet of mosaic, marble or fresco, as were most private houses of any pretension. But the cities did not all look alike. Local traditions, as well as the availability of building materials, ensured a great variety. In the west many cities reflected their origins as Roman colonies by being centered on a forum with its temple to the three gods of the Roman Capitoline, its basilica and senate house, while in the east the Greek tradition of a marketplace which was also the civic center was still dominant at the beginning of the period. During late antiquity, however, the colonnaded street with shops, public buildings and houses behind it became predominant in the eastern provinces. Environmental conditions also made a great difference, dictating the thatched roofs of Britain or the solid stone houses of Syria, the enormous brick and concrete structures of Rome and the marble streets and monuments of Asia Minor.

The buildings, like the society, changed with time as well as space. By the time of Justinian Africa had become a land of small fortresses instead of cities, and urban life had contracted in most other regions. Public monuments often fell into ruin, or were built over with small and crowded houses, foreshadowing a situation which would soon become universal. At the same time, a new and more splendid architecture adorned the cities with monuments which would have formed a striking contrast with the increasing squalor. Some regions, like Cilicia and northern Syria, formed an exception and still preserve clear evidence of their prosperity at the end of the period.

The monuments in general provide information which is rarely available from the historical sources. By showing how the people lived, and by illustrating a great variety of conditions, they make the life of the age more comprehensible and resolve the apparently simple mosaic of late antiquity into innumerable and highly varied tesserae.

The City of Ephesus

Under the Romans, Ephesus was the greatest city in Asia Minor and one of the most important ports of the empire, as well as a center of administration, commerce and finance. Its fine harbor, at the end of a trade route which ran to the eastern frontier, and its hinterland, rich in agriculture and minerals, assured growth and prosperity, while the famous temple of Artemis, one of the seven wonders of the ancient world, attracted visitors from every corner of the empire. In 263 an invasion of the Goths destroyed the temple and did severe damage to the harbor district, but recovery came after peace was restored by Diocletian.

The late antique literary sources – historians, biographers, Church Fathers and others – reveal the continuing importance of the city as a seat of government, trade, communication and religion, but provide few details to reveal the character of urban life. For that, the results of 80 years of excavation are of primary importance. Most of the site was covered with alluvium and silt washed down from the neighboring hillside, so that the first excavator, the Englishman J. T. Wood, had to search long and hard to find the temple in 1873. Since then, much of the site has been cleared and examined in detail, providing an insight into the life of late antiquity which would otherwise be unattainable, and, at the same time, illustrating the value of archaeology for the study of the period.

The location and resources of Ephesus ensured its continuing importance in late antiquity, while the discovery of the tomb of St John the Evangelist on the hill above the ruined temple of Artemis gave it the religious renown among Christians which it had enjoyed in the pagan world. Its fame in this respect was only increased by the knowledge that the Virgin Mary had ascended into heaven from Ephesus and confirmed by the miraculous awakening of the Seven Sleepers in one of the cemeteries of the city. The choice of Ephesus as the site of two councils of the Church, in 430 and 449, illustrates the importance of its strategic location and Christian traditions. Justinian, in recognition of this, crowned the city with a magnificent church dedicated to the Evangelist.

The wealth of late antique Ephesus has been revealed by the excavations in the discovery of numerous buildings erected or rebuilt. The public buildings and services which had characterized the ancient city were maintained, and new ones, such as hospitals and poorhouses, added by the philanthropy of the Church.

At the same time, the appearance of the city underwent a gradual change as a Christian stamp was imposed – vast new churches replaced the temples which were allowed to fall into ruin – and as fashions changed. The great open marketplaces of antiquity, for example, yielded to rows of shops built along the main streets, which became the centers of urban life. Similarly, the huge exercise grounds of the gymnasia tended to be abandoned, leaving, however, the public baths to continue their functions.

This vital and flourishing prosperity was typical of the cities of the eastern provinces in late antiquity and has been similarly revealed by excavations in many other places. At Ephesus, as elsewhere, it came to a sudden end in the early 7th century. In about 614 the central city area was destroyed, apparently by the Persians, and never rebuilt.

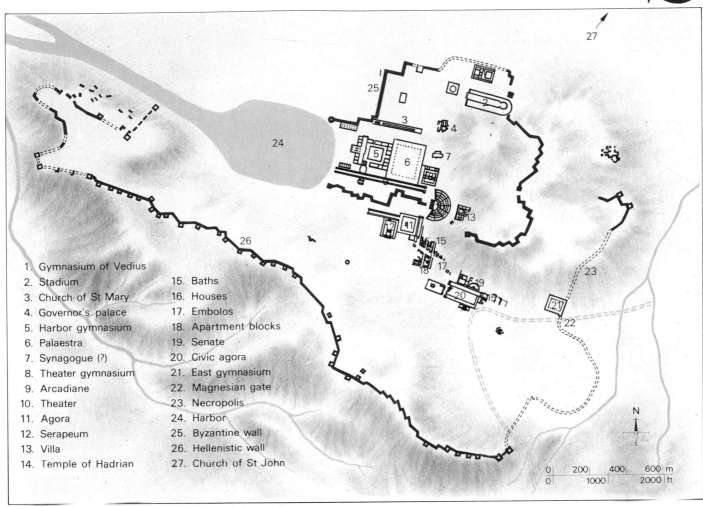

1. Gymnasium of Vedius
2. Stadium
3. Church of St Mary
4. Governor's palace
5. Harbor gymnasium
6. Palaestra
7. Synagogue (?)
8. Theater gymnasium
9. Arcadiane
10. Theater
11. Agora
12. Serapeum
13. Villa
14. Temple of Hadrian
15. Baths
16. Houses
17. Embolos
18. Apartment blocks
19. Senate
20. Civic agora
21. East gymnasium
22. Magnesian gate
23. Necropolis
24. Harbor
25. Byzantine wall
26. Hellenistic wall
27. Church of St John

Above: the site of Ephesus. The Roman and late antique city was built below and between two hills, with the temple of Artemis and church of St John a mile to the northeast. Note that much of the late antique city was left outside the Byzantine walls of the 7th or 8th century.

Left: the harbor district, looking toward the theater. Some of the major late antique buildings lay by the harbor, which has now become a swamp. The theater was rebuilt by governors of the 5th century to serve both for the mimes and pantomimes then favored, and for public meetings.

Above: the boulevard named for the Emperor Arcadius. This construction of the early 5th century is one of the most grandiose examples of urban planning in the provinces. The marble-paved street, called the Arcadiane, stretched 500 yards from the central square by the theater to the harbor. The colonnades, which bore lamps for night lighting, provided shade and protection from the elements; behind them were rows of shops. The larger column in the background is one of four which supported statues of the four Evangelists, a work of Justinian.

Center: the baths of Constantius II. The large baths by the harbor, destroyed by the Goths, were restored in the mid-4th century and given the name of the reigning emperor. New work consisted of adding an oval court which gave access from the Arcadiane; it was paved with marble and elaborately decorated. In the typical style of the age, ancient remains were freely incorporated: the frieze with bulls' heads and wreaths (*far right*) is Classical.

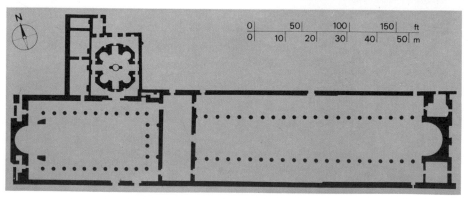

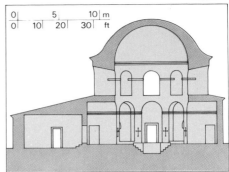

Above and left: the baptistery of St Mary: standing remains and restoration (after Knoll). Late antique cathedrals normally had attached baptisteries, which were especially important in the early period to accommodate the vast numbers of new converts. The plan, as here represented, was derived from that of the hot room of a bath – a domed chamber with a basin recessed in the floor for the total immersion then practiced. The great crosses in relief were probably intended to keep away demons who might interfere at this crucial point in a Christian's life.

Left and opposite below: the church of St Mary. The cathedral church of Ephesus, site of the two councils, was built in the late 4th century in the western part of a huge market basilica which had been ruined by the Goths. Somewhat over half the original structure 280 yards long was used for the church with its long colonnaded *atrium*; part of the rest became the bishop's palace. The great church was eventually ruined and replaced by a smaller domed brick structure in the Dark Ages. That in turn yielded to a still smaller shrine built between the apses of the first and second churches. By that time, the rest of the building was in ruins and a small bath had been built in the *atrium*. Plan after Krautheimer.

Below: the church of St John: the interior, as preserved, and (*bottom*) in restoration (after Hörmann). One of the great monuments of the reign of Justinian, the church was built over the tomb of the Evangelist, preserved below the high altar. In plan it was a domed cruciform basilica of imposing proportions. The interior was decorated with mosaics showing scenes of the Old and New Testaments, the governor receiving his office from an archangel, the emperor dedicating the spoils of war, and Justinian and Theodora crowned by St John. Much of the church has been restored by the benefice of an American millionaire to whom the Evangelist appeared in a dream.

Right: a residential block on the Embolos. Two blocks of houses in the center of the city, now being cleared of the debris which has covered them since the 7th century, are so well preserved that Ephesus is becoming virtually an eastern Pompeii. The blocks contain apartments of varying sizes built on a terraced hillside above the Embolos. They were entered from narrow side streets and preserve much lavish decoration – marble floors, walls with frescoes and mosaics, elegant peristyle courtyards – which reveals a comfortable standard of living. The houses were continually rebuilt and redecorated from the time of Diocletian through that of Justinian. They were destroyed *c*. 614 and never reoccupied.

Opposite center: the Embolos, center of late antique Ephesus. The marble street, which stretched from the marketplace to the civic center, was the busiest place in the city. Its colonnades, lined with statues of emperors, governors and other benefactors, gave access to shops, houses, baths and fountains, and provided a comfortable resort for the people who scratched graffiti and carved game-boards (like the one shown *left*) on the marble pavement. At the top of the street a late antique arch was inscribed with an invocation of the good fortune of the city; the former temple of Hadrian (*center*) was remodeled in the time of Diocletian and decorated with statues of the Tetrarchs. The space behind the colonnade in the foreground was paved with mosaic. Note the extensive reuse of material – hardly any two columns or bases are alike.

Opposite below: a view of the Embolos looking toward the Magnesian Gate.

The Byzantine fortress. The fort was originally designed to protect the church and the bishop, who, as in most cities, became the chief municipal official. It soon became the center of the medieval city which in times of peace stretched outside its walls. The inner citadel (*above*) was added by the Laskarids in the 13th century, when the area enjoyed a burst of prosperity, and numerous fortifications were built against the Turkish threat. In the foreground is the 14th-century Isa Bey Mosque.

Below: the entrance gate built in the Dark Ages with a facade of marble, much of it reused from the nearby temple of Artemis.

4.The Byzantine Age

The Dark Ages, 641–842 AD. The Persian invasions of the early 7th century inaugurated a period of Byzantine history which can very conveniently be called the Dark Ages. During this period the empire was under constant attack from the Arabs who made Asia Minor a perpetual battleground and on two occasions threatened Constantinople itself, as well as from northern neighbors who carried their ravages right up to the walls of the capital. Society was in a continuous state of military alert. Urban civilization virtually ceased to exist outside Constantinople and Thessalonica. Even here, such education as survived was pressed into the service of the religious controversies that were consequent upon so many external disasters. As a result, our knowledge of what went on in Byzantium at this very crucial time is provided by schematic and partisan monastic chronicles, supplemented by saints' lives, coins, a few documents and inscriptions, and the important evidence of archaeology.

The capacity of the Eastern Roman Empire to weather the storm was in great measure due to the efforts of Heraclius and his descendants, who ruled the empire for nearly a century and constituted the first real Byzantine dynasty. The Heraclians had a tendency to be autocratic and uncompromising, which led them to commit serious faults. Thus Heraclius and his grandson Constans II (641–68) made themselves unpopular by trying to impose a theological doctrine akin to the Monophysite heresy. Constans' idea of transferring the government to Syracuse was damaging to public morale. His son Constantine IV (668–85) by an ill-considered expedition (680) allowed the Bulgars, a Turkic tribe who had appeared on the northern frontier, to gain mastery of the Slavs south of the Danube and thus to constitute a permanent threat to imperial security in the Balkans. Constantine's son Justinian II ruled with an unbridled tyranny which brought him to ten years in exile (695–705) and to a violent end in 711, at a time when the state most desperately needed to present a united front to the Arabs. Yet the descendants of Heraclius effectively prevented the Arabs from taking Asia Minor and from gaining a decisive advantage at sea: in the 670s the Byzantine forces so successfully broke a sustained attempt to take Constantinople from bases in Asia Minor that the Arab ruler Moawiya, formerly governor and now caliph at Damascus, agreed to pay tribute to Constantine IV. The most lasting and fundamental achievement of the Heraclians was to transform Byzantium into a society geared for war. The empire was divided into a number of military zones called *themes*, in which the commanding officer was also the civil administrator. The *theme* system was extended and modified by later rulers; in essentials it endured until the end of the 11th century. After a series of ephemeral emperors succeeded Justinian II, the general

The iconodule view of iconoclasm. Top: the Patriarch Nikephoros and the leader of the monastic party, Theodore the Studite, hold an image of Christ. Corner: Theodore disputes with an iconoclast patriarch in the presence of an iconoclast emperor. Right: iconoclast bishops spear an image of Christ. British Library, Add. MS 19352.

Leo III came to the throne in 717, just four months before the Arabs launched their attack, a land and sea operation on a massive scale. Once again "Greek fire" was used to good effect, but the Arab defeat was ultimately brought about by factors outside Byzantine control: the unusually severe winter of 717–18, the depletion of the Arab stores, a Bulgar attack which killed 20,000 of the besiegers, and a storm which destroyed the greater part of their fleet as it withdrew. The caliph's land forces retreated in fairly good order, and soon returned to the offensive in Asia Minor. Not until Leo and his son Constantine won a decisive victory in 739 was this offensive seriously checked. However, the Arab attempt to dominate Europe had failed, and as if to symbolize this failure, the Umayyad caliphate of Damascus collapsed in the mid-8th century. The new Abbasid caliphate of Baghdad was more remote from Byzantium, and more disposed to accept coexistence with the Christian empire. The Byzantines were still to suffer some of their worst humiliations at Arab hands, but these did not occur as part of a systematic advance on Constantinople.

Previous page: the Emperor Constantine IV giving privileges to the archbishop of Ravenna with his brothers Heraclius and Tiberius standing next to him and, on the far left, his son Justinian II. St Apollinare in Classe, Ravenna; mosaic on the north wall of the apse.

Iconoclasm and schism. The reigns of Leo III (717–41), Constantine V (741–75) and Leo IV (775–80) constitute the second great dynastic succession in Byzantium. Leo III and Constantine V were among the ablest Byzantine emperors. Constantine performed feats against the Bulgarian kingdom which were no less valuable for the security of the state than those of his father against the Arabs. Leo III made a name for himself as a legislator by publishing the *Ecloga*, a law code which contained some notable departures from that of Justinian, but which was primarily intended as a workable substitute for earlier manuals. For all their talents, however, these two emperors were execrated in later Byzantine memory because they had attempted to abolish the veneration of icons, painted representations of Christ and the saints. In 726–27 Leo delivered sermons against icon-worship and took down an icon of Christ from over the Bronze Gate to the imperial palace. This incident caused riots in the capital, but Leo was not deterred from promulgating an edict ordering all icons to be destroyed (730). Serious opposition followed his death, when his son-in-law Artavasdus used iconodule support (i.e. favoring icon-worship) to have himself proclaimed emperor in Constantinople. Constantine V defeated Artavasdus in 743. For the rest of his reign he imposed iconoclasm with a zeal far surpassing that of Leo. In 754 he convened an iconoclast council at Hieria outside Constantinople. After this, destruction of icons was widespread, accompanied by cruel persecution of monks: measures which earned Constantine the name Kopronymos – "named of excrement."

The iconoclast policy of Leo and Constantine was opposed by the popes, and contributed to the estrangement of the old from the new Rome. In 751 Ravenna, for three centuries the center of a Byzantine exarchate, fell to the Lombards, and with it all that was left of Byzantine power in northern and central Italy. Shortly afterwards, the emperor transferred the ecclesiastical provinces of Sicily, Calabria and Illyricum in the Balkans, from the jurisdiction of Rome to that of Constantinople.

Constantine's son Leo IV was a more moderate iconoclast than his father. He had a fanatically iconodule wife, Irene, who after his untimely death in 780 took over the regency for their young son Constantine VI. In 784 Irene secured the election of an iconodule patriarch, Tarasios, and in 787 delegates from all over the Christian world met at Nicaea to form a council which reinstated icons as objects of divine intercession. Yet many former agents of Constantine V remained at large and unrepentant. The young Constantine VI, chafing under his mother's tutelage, conspired with them to have her removed, and although she soon returned, he ruled for a while as senior partner. But he alienated all support by cruelly mutilating members of his family, by turning against his iconoclast followers, and by forming a bigamous relationship. In 797 Irene had her son blinded. For five years she ruled as sole empress. Yet she failed to improve upon a foreign situation which had been growing worse since the death of Constantine V, and actually contributed to it by remitting taxes to gain popularity. Byzantium was unfortunate to be ruled by her inept government of eunuchs at a time when Italy came under the sway of Charlemagne, king of the Franks, and Pope Leo III showed his gratitude to this new protector by crowning him emperor at Rome on Christmas Day 800, thus challenging the Byzantine claim to universal Christian sovereignty. In 802 a palace revolution banished Irene from Constantinople, and elevated a treasury official to be the emperor Nikephoros I.

Nikephoros was responsible for taxation measures, administrative reforms and transfers of population which much restored the internal strength of the empire, although they were thoroughly unpopular with the monks, whose hatred is fully expressed by the contemporary chronicler Theophanes. Perhaps the most notable achievement of the reign was the initiation of an expansionist policy in mainland Greece. For two centuries Byzantine power had been restricted to a few fortified coastal cities; now a systematic attempt seems to have been made to subdue and Christianize the Slavs of the interior.

In his other foreign relations, Nikephoros was less successful. He left the question of Charlemagne's title unresolved. The death in 809 of the great Abbasid Caliph Harun-al-Rashid afforded him some relief on his eastern frontier. But in the Balkans he faced, from 805, the most formidable Bulgarian ruler who had yet taken the field against Byzantium: Krum. In 809 Krum captured the important Byzantine outpost of Serdica (modern Sofia). By 811 his raids were becoming so intolerable that Nikephoros led a huge expedition into Bulgaria which destroyed Krum's capital of Pliska, but was crushed near Serdica. Nikephoros was slain in his tent – the first emperor since Valens to fall in battle – and Krum fashioned a drinking-goblet from his skull.

The patriarch soon crowned the late emperor's son-in law, Michael Rhangabe, whose one positive achievement was the recognition of Charlemagne's imperial status in terms which were minimally damaging to Byzantium. After another disastrous confrontation with Krum in 813, Michael resigned and went into exile; his place was taken by Leo, general of the Anatolikon *theme*.

Leo came to power with the support of the strong iconoclast element in the army, whose disaffection had contributed to recent disasters, and he began to enforce a moderate ban on icons. In 820 he was murdered at a service in St Sophia, and replaced by his former companion in arms, Michael of Amorion.

Michael II (820–29), also a moderate iconoclast, was immediately faced by the revolt of his former companion in arms, Thomas "the Slav," who laid siege to Constantinople after devastating Asia Minor, and was not defeated until 823. Michael owed his victory to the intervention of the Bulgar ruler Omurtag, the successor of Krum who had died in 814 after a last campaign of destruction in revenge for a treacherous attempt on his life by Leo V. In spite of this relief, Michael II was not able to deal successfully with his other enemies: about 826 a group of Spanish Arabs operating from Egypt captured the island of Crete, and a year later the Muslims began the systematic conquest of Sicily.

Michael's son Theophilos (829–42) did little to improve the foreign situation, and maintained iconoclasm at home. Yet being an educated man, with exotic tastes in art and a passion for justice, he symbolized the emergence of the empire from a period when the ruler had to be a soldier into one where he had time to cultivate the arts of peace.

The Dark Ages produced some large and important monuments, of types characteristic of the Byzantine age – fortresses and churches. The great invasions naturally produced a network of powerful fortresses in the previously peaceful lands of Asia Minor. Notable among them are the fortifications of Ancyra and of Cotyaeum, the rebuilding of the walls of Nicaea, and a series of fortresses in western Asia Minor – Sardis, Pergamum, Ephesus, Miletus and others – where large city sites were abandoned and the reduced population retreated behind the shelter of heavy walls protecting a much smaller area.

The same period produced a series of churches, some quite large and elaborate, important in the development of Byzantine architecture. These domed basilicas, mostly built of brick, represent a transitional stage in the development of the cross-in-square church, and include the rebuilding of St Irene in the capital, St Sophia in Thessalonica, and a group in Asia Minor: the Koimesis at Nicaea (now destroyed), St Mary at Ephesus, the church at Sige in Bithynia, St Nicholas in Myra, and the monastery of Dere Ağzi in Lycia. Buildings of Constantinople will be considered separately below.

The straitened circumstances of the time, when what resources were left to the empire had necessarily to be devoted to physical and spiritual defense, precluded the construction of the secular and public buildings which characterized late antiquity, and with the decline of city life many of these were hardly necessary or appropriate. Secular building would not reappear on a large scale outside Constantinople until the end of the Byzantine age.

The great age of Byzantium, 843–1025. The iconoclast policy of Michael and Theophilos had not brought religious unity to the empire. Public opinion now favored a restoration of icons, and this was effected in 843 when Theodora, the emperor's widow and regent for their young son Michael III, called a synod which reintroduced the decrees of the council of 787. The issue was not raised again. How far iconoclasm had stifled the cultural life of Byzantium is hard to say. But the art, architecture and learning which can truly be called Byzantine have their beginnings in the mid-9th century. The century and a half following the death of Theophilos was also the period in which Byzantium attained its greatest military strength.

This period of greatness is traditionally associated with the "Macedonian" dynasty, although it should be noted that it began with the reign of Michael III, and that of the four great soldier-emperors of the 10th century only one was a descendant of Basil I, "the Macedonian."

The regime of Theodora was notable for a renewal of war with the caliphate, in which Byzantium began to improve its position, and for the large-scale persecution of the Paulicians, a heretical group in western Asia Minor whose hostile treatment at the hands of the Byzantines had caused them to support the Arabs. Theodora made the mistake of dictating to her son, and in 856 Michael, with the aid of her brother Bardas, deposed her and became head of state, although the government was handled by Bardas, who received the title of Caesar, and his brother Petronas. Their administration was one of the most successful that Byzantium ever had. Although the Byzantines continued to lose ground in Sicily, they turned to the attack in Asia Minor, and in 863 Petronas won a great victory against the emir of Melitene.

Bardas was keenly aware of the value of culture in politics. At home he encouraged education, and abroad he organized the first attempts to convert the Slavs to Orthodox Christianity. In 860 the empire had its first encounter with the Ros, the Viking rulers of the Slavs of Russia, when a Russian fleet appeared in the Bosphorus. From this point dates the long series of Byzantine missionary efforts in Russia. More immediate results were achieved among the Slavs of central Europe and Bulgaria.

Here the Byzantine missionaries were directed by two exceptionally able brothers from Thessalonica, Cyril and Methodius who facilitated conversion by creating for the Slavs a religious literature in their own language. At the head of the Byzantine Church was Photios, a man of great learning, idealism and political shrewdness. His patriarchate was a stormy one. He had been appointed by Bardas in the coup of 856 to replace Ignatios, a simple monk who represented the Church's "zealot" faction. This faction objected to the fact of Photios having been a layman prior to his appointment, and its complaints were taken up in Rome, where Pope Nicholas I was anxious to outbid the Byzantines for the "contract" of converting Bulgaria. Nicholas in 863 declared the patriarch deposed and Ignatios restored. In 867 Photios replied by holding a synod which excommunicated the pope and pronounced the Roman Church heretical. This schism was exacerbated by the fact that Boris of Bulgaria had decided that Rome could offer him Christianity on more favorable terms.

Meanwhile, the political government of the empire was being upset by violent changes. Michael III adopted as his favorite Basil, a young peasant from Byzantine Macedonia, who so gained the emperor's affections that he was able to murder Bardas (865) and have himself crowned coemperor (866). He completed his rise to power the next year by murdering his benefactor.

Basil immediately deposed Photios, restored Ignatios

A coin of Leo VI (886–912), nicknamed "the Wise" for his many literary works and law code. Dumbarton Oaks.

and resumed relations with Rome. In other matters, however, he hardly deviated from the policies of the previous reign. The pope was allowed no further jurisdiction in Constantinople, and Bulgaria was reclaimed for the Byzantine Church by the adoption of a more conciliatory attitude. Basil also extended Byzantine influence in the western Balkan area, converting the Slavs in the Adriatic hinterland and asserting his sovereignty in Dalmatia. There were some early setbacks in southern Italy, which almost succumbed to the Arabs, and was saved by Charlemagne's grandson Louis II, who felt encouraged to defy Byzantium and call himself emperor of the Romans. But Basil won the confidence of the local Lombard princes, and in 876 the Byzantines reestablished themselves in the important coastal city of Bari. A few years later an outstanding general, Nikephoros Phokas, arrived to conduct an offensive which confirmed Byzantine hegemony south of Rome. The Arabs were masters of the sea, and in 878 they took Syracuse. Yet Byzantine power revived sufficiently for Basil to be feared and his protection welcomed by the pope. At the death of Ignatios in 877, Photios returned to the patriarchate with no protest from Rome, and remained there until Basil's death in 886.

Basil was succeeded by his son Leo VI (886–912), nicknamed "the Wise" for his large number of literary works, as well as a law code, the *Basilica*, the foundations for which had been laid by his father, and which effectively replaced the Justinianic compilations as a handbook of Byzantine law. It was in Leo's reign that the imperial bureaucracy reached the height of its development, and that imperial absolutism in state and Church received fullest expression.

Leo made great efforts to strengthen the army and navy, but the results were not apparent during his reign. Byzantium now entered upon its most terrible struggle with the Bulgars. In 894 the tsar Symeon declared war when Leo permitted measures which diminished the profits of the Bulgarian export trade. Leo temporarily neutralized Symeon by calling upon the nomadic Magyars, who then lived in the areas north and northwest of the Black Sea, to attack Bulgaria in the rear. But Symeon countered this move by allying with the Pechenegs, the next tribe to the east, who caused great destruction among their neighbors; the remnant of the Magyars founded Hungary. Meanwhile Symeon achieved a victory which enabled him to impose peace terms highly favorable to himself.

The situation in Asia Minor did not change significantly, but at sea the Byzantines suffered some of their worst disasters. In 902 they finally lost Sicily to the Arabs; in the same year the Arabs sacked Demetrias, a rich coastal city in Greece, and two years later a renegade Greek, Leo of Tripoli, plundered Thessalonica, second city in the empire. At home Leo contributed to the internal divisions of the Byzantine Church by making a fourth marriage in spite of the fact that a third was not canonically permissible.

In the confusion which followed Leo's death in 912, Symeon appeared at the gates of Constantinople demanding that he be crowned emperor and that Leo's seven-year-old son and heir Constantine marry one of his daughters. These demands were refused by Zoe, Leo's fourth wife and Constantine's mother, when she and her "administration of eunuchs" took over the regency. Symeon ravaged all the Byzantine territories in Europe. A huge expedition sent against him in 917 met with disaster on the Black Sea coast. This called for a change of government. The leader of the fleet, Romanos Lekapenos, by degrees triumphed over all rivals and had himself proclaimed emperor (920).

Consolidation of the empire. By arranging for Constantine VII to marry his daughter he appeared not to usurp the rights of the legitimate dynasty, and by calling a synod to have fourth marriages declared illegal he restored unity to the Church. Himself a born statesman, and served by men of genius, Romanos had one of the most constructive reigns in Byzantine history. His accession frustrated the designs of Symeon of Bulgaria, who continued to seek revenge until his death in 927. From this point, however, the Byzantine armies were free to take the offensive in Asia Minor. The organizational work of Leo VI was now matched by brilliant leadership in the field. Under the general John Kourkouas, the eastern armies gained victory after victory against the Arab emirates of Armenia and Cilicia, culminating in the siege of Edessa (944), in which that city's prize relic – a cloth on which Christ had left the imprint of His face – was transferred in triumph to Constantinople. Shortly before this, in 941, the Byzantines had heavily defeated a new expedition against Constantinople by the Russians of Kiev.

In 944 Romanos was deposed by his own sons, who were annoyed that he had not given them preference over Constantine VII. It was, however, Constantine the "Porphyrogenitos" – i.e. the legitimate ruler, "born in the purple chamber of the palace" – who reaped the benefit of their coup. Although Constantine had been on the throne for 33 years, he had been kept very much in the background, and had consoled himself with reading, writing and painting. His own reign was not notable for any military achievement. Yet his treatise on foreign relations reveals a good theoretical grasp of diplomacy, and his dealings with other monarchs show that this knowledge did not lack practical application. The treatise and another which he composed on court ceremonial are major evidence for the Byzantine conception of empire.

Constantine was briefly succeeded by his son Romanos II (959–63). The armed forces were now led by Nikephoros Phokas, the most distinguished of a long line of soldier aristocrats. In 961 he succeeded, where every emperor since Theophilos had failed, in recapturing Crete from its Arab masters. The next year he finally defeated the chief Byzantine enemy in the east, the emir of Aleppo Saif-ad-Daulah. When Romanos died, his widow Theophano invited Nikephoros to share power with her.

The new emperor was obsessed with the war against Islam, and continued the Byzantine drive to the east with ever-increasing speed; by 969 Antioch belonged to the empire. In other respects, Nikephoros II was less successful: he treated the newly revived Western Empire of Otto the Saxon with a contempt which endangered the Byzantine possessions in southern Italy; in attempting to use the Russians of Kiev to punish the Bulgars, he allowed their prince, Svjatoslav, to gain influence in Bulgaria; and

Joshua portrayed as the victorious Byzantine soldier of the 10th century: fresco in the church of Hosios Loukas near Delphi.

he lost the support of Theophano, and his best general, John Tzimiskes, both of whom conspired at the end of 969 to have him murdered.

Tzimiskes, who now became emperor, belonged to the same military aristocratic class as his predecessor. In western affairs he showed himself more competent: he crushingly defeated the combined forces of Svjatoslav and the Bulgars (971), and appeased Otto the Great by sending his kinswoman Theophano to marry the German emperor's son (972). But like Nikephoros II, his ambitions lay on the eastern front. His armies swept through Syria and Palestine, and they might have gone much further had he not died of typhoid in January 976.

The successes of the 10th century had not only given the military, territorial aristocracy of Asia Minor high social prestige, but also had brought two of their outstanding representatives to the throne. At the death of John Tzimiskes, his brother-in-law, Bardas Skleros, was ready to take his place and to push into the background the legitimate "Macedonian" heirs Basil and Constantine, the sons of Romanos II and Theophano. But Basil was not disposed to accept such treatment. Thanks to his great-uncle Basil, a eunuch and illegitimate son of Romanos Lekapenos who had served the last three emperors, he was able to use another aristocratic general, Bardas Phokas, to defeat Skleros and force him to take refuge in Baghdad (979). Six years later Basil II exiled his great-uncle on a charge of treason and took the government into his own hands.

Tzimiskes' campaign against Svjatoslav of Kiev had brought all Bulgaria under Byzantine rule, but after his death a revolt broke out and Samuel of Macedonia proclaimed himself tsar and established his capital at Ochrid; gradually almost the whole Balkan area came under his sway. In 985–86 Basil II led a counteroffensive but was badly beaten. The defeat led to the disaffection of the military aristocracy; in 987 Bardas Skleros and Bardas Phokas again led revolts which were only put down with the assistance of the Russian prince Vladimir, to whom Basil promised his sister in marriage. Peace was restored in 989 and the marriage between Vladimir and Basil's sister Anna took place shortly afterwards; with it went the conversion of the Kievan state to Christianity, and the organization of its Church under Byzantine direction.

Basil spent the rest of his life in fighting the empire's enemies. He made three memorable appearances on the eastern front, in which Syria was pacified and Armenia occupied. But his life's work was the destruction of Samuel and the new Bulgarian empire. He began a systematic offensive in 1001, aimed at cleaving Samuel's state in two, and then reducing the western part, where the enemy was based. The bitter fighting of the next decade ended in the complete annihilation of Samuel's army at a battle near Prilep in the Struma valley. Although Samuel managed to escape, he died of grief two days later when his army returned to him blinded. By 1018 Basil had eliminated the last pockets of resistance. The whole area south of the rivers Sava and Danube now came under Byzantine rule; Bulgaria and Macedonia were integrated with the provincial administration of the empire.

At his death in 1025, Basil II left the Byzantine Empire greater than it had been at any time since the reign of Justinian I, and this was largely his own personal achievement. Unlike almost every other emperor, he ruled entirely by his own will and not by cooperation with some powerful internal interest. The revolts of the early part of his reign made him determined to exclude the military aristocracy from dominating positions, and his visits to Asia Minor convinced him that he needed to strike at the economic basis of this class's power. Romanos Lekapenos and Constantine VII had legislated against the process by which the aristocracy was acquiring peasant small-holdings, a process which diminished both the taxable and the military potential of the peasantry. Basil II extended

The Ninazan Kilise, a rock-cut church near Macan in Cappadocia. Frescoes in these churches are perhaps the finest evidence of the 10th-century flowering of monasticism.

their legislation and applied it with greater severity and effect: according to the letter of the law as laid down by him, much aristocratic property was declared illegal and reverted to the state. Basil governed the bureaucracy and the Church with an equally iron hand.

The prosperity of the dynamic age of the Macedonians is reflected in the great number of churches and monasteries which were built. The great age of construction of fortresses had already taken place, and to their number relatively few were added: the rebuilding of the walls of Nicaea and Ancyra by Michael III and of Attalia by Leo VI are striking examples of the defensive architecture of the period which generally continued the work of the Dark Ages and extended it into the newly won regions.

Widespread peace gave monasticism the security it needed to flourish. In the late 10th century the most famous of Byzantine monastic complexes, that of Mount

Athos, was founded, and many others grew in Greece and Asia Minor: Hosios Loukas in central Greece, Daphni near Athens and Nea Moni in Chios, all decorated with splendid mosaics of the 11th century, and the rock cut churches of Cappadocia with their frescoes are perhaps the most outstanding examples of this extensive phenomenon.

Church building in towns and villages was extremely active, beginning in the late 9th century with the Nea in the capital (now destroyed), Skripou in Boeotia and the churches of Triglea in Bithynia. The age saw the almost universal fashion of the cross-in-square church of which several fine examples are visible in Athens, Thessalonica, Rhodes, Cyprus and, on a small scale, in Kastoria. In Asia Minor the two outstanding monuments of Çanli Kilise and Üç Ayak, both in Cappadocia, date from the period.

The collapse and the Komnenian revival, 1025–1180.

The greatness of Byzantium under Basil II was so dependent upon the emperor that the series of ineffectual monarchs who ruled for the half-century after his death reduced the state to a condition from which it never properly recovered. These emperors, who mostly represented the interests of the educated bureaucrats at Constantinople, were able, thanks to Basil, to keep the military aristocracy at arm's length, yet they lacked the authority to enforce Basil's land legislation, and they themselves were completely unable to supply any military initiative. As a result, the great conquests of the past century were undone, and the empire was threatened on all fronts. A band of Norman adventurers was able to turn against the Byzantines and seize southern Italy from the empire. The Pechenegs, followed by other Turkic tribes from the steppes, broke across the Danube and ravaged the Balkans and Greece. In the east, the warlike Turkish dynasty of Seljuk had taken over the Muslim empire of Baghdad. In 1071 the Seljuk ruler Alp Arslan defeated a large Byzantine army under the command of the emperor Romanos IV at Manzikert in Armenia. In the enfeebled circumstances of the empire at this time, such a defeat was a disaster. It exposed the whole of Asia Minor to Turkish attacks. By 1080 the Turks controlled all but the coastal areas, and had founded a sultanate at Iconium in the center of Anatolia. Asia Minor had supplied the empire with food and soldiers for many centuries. There could be no substitute for it, and it was never effectively recovered.

By the middle of the century it was clear that only an emperor who enjoyed the support of the military aristocracy could save the state. The situation was desperate when, in 1810, the right candidate at last presented himself: Alexios Komnenos. At home he inherited a depleted treasury, a demoralized army and a non-existent navy. Abroad he had hardly a foothold in Asia Minor, and the Normans, now masters of Sicily as well as southern Italy, were attacking the Byzantine possessions across the Adriatic. Alexios tried to deal with this threat first. He

Above: the church of Üç Ayak in Cappadocia. This fine church, built of brick in an elaborate technique developed in the Macedonian period, may have been constructed to celebrate the victory of Basil II over the rebel Bardas Phokas.

Top: Constantine IX Monomachos, commemorated for his generosity to the Church in a gallery of St Sophia. The mosaic originally represented the Emperor Romanos III Argyros (1028–34); his face and inscription were changed, but the Empress Zoe (wife of both men) remains on the right.

Opposite: a monastic landscape: the Ilhara valley in Cappadocia. Invisible from the surrounding countryside, this valley provided an abode for numerous monks, who carved their churches and chapels in the soft rock faces of the cliffs during the Macedonian period.

pawned Church plate in order to raise what troops he could, and he enlisted maritime aid from Venice at the price of allowing the Italian republic trade concessions in Byzantine ports which even his own subjects did not enjoy. These measures did not prevent the Normans from taking the important coastal city of Dyrrachion, and it was only the death, in 1085, of their king Robert Guiscard which effectively frustrated their strategy.

Now the Pechenegs posed a threat. With the aid of Tzachas, a Turkish emir who had established himself in Smyrna, they besieged Constantinople in 1090–91. Resorting to the time-honored Byzantine diplomatic trick

of inciting distant powers to attack the enemy in the rear, Alexios set the Cumans against the Pechenegs and another Turk against Tzachas. In 1091 the combined Byzantine and Cuman forces annihilated a whole Pecheneg tribe; in 1094 the emperor defeated a Cuman invasion led by a Byzantine pretender.

At this point, when Alexios could have taken the offensive in Asia Minor, his plans were affected by the beginning of the crusading movement in the west. The Turkish capture of the Holy Sepulcher (1077) had focused the expansionism now prevalent in western Europe. In 1096 Pope Urban II preached the First Crusade, and the next year its leaders assembled in Constantinople. Alexios managed to bind most of them to himself by feudal oaths, and they did him the favor of taking Nicaea; after this, he recovered western Asia Minor. But as soon as the crusaders were established in Palestine, some of them quarreled with the emperor, notably Bohemond, the son of Robert Guiscard. Fortunately, Alexios was able to defeat a new attempt to attack Byzantium from the west (1107).

Alexios' son John II (1118–43) continued the process of recovery with unfailing success. He pacified the Serbs, inflicted a final defeat on the Pechenegs and restored Byzantine influence in southeastern Asia Minor. After his premature death in 1143, his son Manuel inherited a situation so promising that the new ruler felt encouraged to behave as if the empire had regained all its old strength. Manuel was a clever diplomat and a competent soldier. His foreign policy was on the same scale as his lavish, cosmopolitan court, and in Hungary and the crusader states of the east it achieved some notable successes. In all other areas, however, it was a magnificent failure. An attempt to dominate the east coast of Italy was defeated by a hostile coalition of western powers, including the newly aggressive German empire of Frederick I Barbarossa, and did not make up for the Norman sack of Corinth and Thebes. After years of skilled diplomacy had failed to yield anything but promises from the Turkish rulers of Anatolia, an expedition against them was heavily defeated at Myriokephalon (1176).

The Komnenoi could not indeed hope to recreate the empire of Basil II, and their energetic policies depended on measures which weakened the government and made it unpopular: the devaluation of the gold coinage, the use of mercenaries, the sale of offices, the farming of taxes, the granting of state lands in benefice, excessive taxation of many and immunity for a few. Yet the state did acquire a new internal stability. Alexios I, John II and Manuel I not only formed an undisputed dynastic succession, but also, by appointing their relatives to high office and marrying them into other prominent families, they made the name Komnenos a highly prized symbol of social status. They created new titles which allowed a greater number of their intimates to have the sense of sharing in the imperial dignity, and they made the administration more of a "household" affair, dependent on personal ties to the emperor. This closing of the ranks was undoubtedly a defensive measure, but it demonstrates the Byzantines' ability to adapt their timeless ideal to drastic changes of circumstance. Byzantine decline in the 11th and 12th centuries is striking mainly in view of the contemporary rise of Latin Christendom, reflected in the military vigor of the Crusades and the commercial enterprise of the Italian maritime republics – Amalfi, Pisa, Genoa and Venice.

In spite of their great accomplishments, the Komnenoi have left behind few major monuments in the provinces. This is due partly to the precarious nature of their reconquest of Asia Minor, where even the small coastal region they controlled was constantly subject to attack, partly to the hazards of preservation. In Asia Minor their work is visible in the fortifications of Pergamum and in numerous small chapels on the south coast, and in the Balkans in the important churches of Nerezi near Skopje and Pherrai (Bera) near Alexandropolis. In Greece the monastery of Chilandari on Mount Athos belongs to the age, as does the attractive group of small churches with elaborate brick decoration in the Argolid, and various small churches and chapels elsewhere.

The disintegration of the Komnenian empire, the exile and the empire of Nicaea, 1180–1261.

Manuel I died in 1180, leaving his Latin widow Mary to act as regent for their young son Alexios II; however, Manuel's cousin Andronikos now made a bid for the throne by condemning the pro-aristocratic and western tendencies of the previous reign, and was swept to power on a popular wave, in which the mob of Constantinople massacred most of the Latins in the city (1182). Within a very short time the new emperor had rooted out many long-standing abuses in the administration. Yet the means he used to achieve these ends were violent, and provoked violent reactions, especially from the aristocracy. Andronikos now behaved with a ferocious cruelty which alienated his supporters and allowed the defenses of the empire to deteriorate. With Hungarian help, Stephen Nemanja, founder of the medieval kingdom of Serbia, broke free; Cyprus was severed from the empire. The Normans of Sicily marched unopposed from Dyrrachion to Thessalonica, which they took and sacked brutally (1185). This event precipitated Andronikos' downfall, and the crown was offered to Isaac Angelos, a grandson of Alexios I's daughter Theodora.

Isaac II (1185–95) managed to rid the empire of the Normans, but in all other respects the situation deteriorated rapidly under him and under his brother Alexios III (1195–1203) who deposed him. The administrative decay of Manuel's reign resumed with a vengeance, and encouraged a series of revolts throughout the provinces. Most serious of these was a rising in Bulgaria (1186) which led to a revival of the Bulgarian empire. It was only a matter of time before the Latins tried to exploit the situation. Isaac II's son Alexios appealed to the westerners for help against his uncle. The leaders of the Fourth Crusade, which set out in 1203 for Egypt, turned aside to Constantinople and put Alexios IV on the throne. When he was overthrown by a popular revolt, the crusaders took the city by storm (1204). After an appalling sack, they set up a Latin emperor and patriarch, and shared out the provinces.

The Latin empire of Constantinople (1204–61) was an inglorious affair, crippled by succession problems and by a lack of funds which Venice, who had taken the lion's share of the profits, did nothing to remedy. The initiative quickly passed to the empire's Orthodox enemies. The Bulgarian Tsar Kalojan crushed a Latin army at Adrianople (1206) although he soon alienated the Greeks by his excessive savagery. Substantial gains were then made by relatives of the Angelos emperors who had established themselves in Epirus: Michael, and his brother Theodore. Theodore succeeded in expelling the Latins from Macedonia and western Thrace, and proclaimed himself emperor in Thessalonica (1225). However, his empire collapsed in 1230, when he was defeated by the Bulgarians. The future now lay with the empire of Nicaea, which Byzantine refugees had founded in western Asia Minor. The founder of this state, Theodore I Laskaris (1204–22), had beaten off strong offensives by the Latins of Constantinople and by the Turkish sultan. By carrying further Alexios I's "closing of the ranks" of the aristocracy around the emperor, Theodore bequeathed to his son-in-law John III Vatatzes (1222–54) a compact, solvent and militarily efficient patrimony. John, a good soldier and a wise administrator, prevailed against the Latins, the Bulgars and the Greek rulers of the west. He and his son Theodore II (1254–58) extended their sway over Macedonia and Thrace. But it was left to a usurper, Michael VIII Palaiologos, to gain reentry to Contantinople (summer 1261).

The Laskarids did much to promote the security and prosperity of their domains, to which they brought honest and efficient government and half a century of peace. These conditions were propitious for an extensive building program which has left its traces throughout western Asia Minor. The walls of Nicaea were rebuilt with a lower outer wall added, Magnesia, the capital, was given a new rampart, and an extensive network of fortresses was erected throughout their dominions, in a style usually characterized by the decorative use of brick in the stonework. The Laskarids founded two famous monasteries, Lembos near Smyrna and Sosandra near Magnesia, but neither has survived. Only a ruined church at Sardis

Above: remains of the palace at Nymphaeum, near Smyrna, where the emperors of Nicaea frequently resided.

Right: a gold coin of Andronikos II (1282–1328). The decline of the Byzantine economy from 900 to 1300 is apparent when this coin is compared with the one of Leo VI on page 83. Dumbarton Oaks.

reflects their piety. They are responsible, in addition, for one of the few large secular monuments of the age, a well-preserved palace at Nymphaeum, residence of the emperors.

The Palaiologoi and the fall of Byzantium, 1261–1461.

The restored empire faced all the problems which had confronted the Komnenoi and Angeloi, and more. To ensure a naval arm, Michael Palaiologos had had to make enormous concessions to the Genoese (1260). A victory in 1259 had given him a foothold in the Peloponnese from 1262, but the Latins remained strongly entrenched here, in Athens and in the islands; the Greeks of Epirus and Thessaly refused Michael more than a nominal obedience. Even in Macedonia and Thrace, generations of unstable rule had made the town-dwellers half-hearted in their loyalty to anything but their own communal interests. Although Michael followed the example of Alexios Komnenos in making the court a family enterprise, the stain of usurpation attached to his accession, and his cruel blinding of Theodore II's young son John IV caused the first serious schism in the Church that had occurred for centuries. Religious divisions were exacerbated by foreign policy. The Latins were determined not to accept their defeat, and they found a powerful champion in King Charles I of Naples. Michael tried to deprive Charles of papal support by promising to settle his Church's differences with Rome and submit unconditionally to the pope. But for over a century, and especially since the crusaders' sack of Constantinople in 1204, the Byzantine people had felt nothing but loathing for the Latins and their Church. Even Michael's own family opposed the union, and as an instrument of policy it became useless in 1280, when a French pope was elected. Fortunately, Charles's invasion plans were frustrated by a military defeat in Albania (1281) and a revolt in Sicily (1282). In this year Michael VIII died.

The reign of Andronikos II (1282–1328) was one of the periods of most rapid Byzantine decline. All of Asia Minor, apart from the cities of Nicomedia and Philadelphia, was lost to the Turks. Andronikos was not altogether at fault for this; the frontier defense system had been gravely neglected by Michael VIII in his struggle with the west. However, the emperor lacked the will to make the necessary army and land reforms, and the troops at the front demonstrated their attitude by inciting his only commander of genius to unsuccessful rebellion. In 1302 he resorted to a remedy which proved worse than the disease,

Alexios Apokaukos, *megas doux* (1340–45), from a manuscript of
Hippocrates in the Bibliothèque Nationale, Paris.

inviting a company of Catalan mercenaries to fight in Asia
Minor. After some minor victories, the Catalans began to
plunder and extort payment from their employers. From
1304 to 1311 they ravaged Thrace, Macedonia and Thessaly, until they picked a quarrel with the Latins of Greece
and established themselves in Athens and Thebes.

The Empire was soon convulsed by a series of civil
wars. In the 1320s the struggle was between Andronikos
and his grandson and namesake and brought the latter,
as Andronikos III, to supreme power in Constantinople
in 1328.

An expedition against the Turks met with disaster
(1329), but otherwise Andronikos' reign was the brightest
of the Palaiologan dynasty. The emperor defended the
rich islands of Chios and Lesbos against the Genoese, held
the frontier against the Serbs and Bulgars and restored
Epirus and Thessaly to the rule of Constantinople for the
first time since 1204. Yet there were two conspiracies
against him, and tension developed between his powerful
aristocratic confidant John Kantakouzenos and the new
men of his administration. After the emperor's premature
death in 1341, Kantakouzenos proclaimed himself emperor.

The civil war which followed is one of the most
interesting episodes in Byzantine history, since a case can
be made for regarding it as a struggle between social
classes: between the landed aristocracy led by Kantakouzenos, and the suppressed "bourgeoisie" who favored
lower commercial taxes and the maintenance of a strong
fleet to allow competition with the Venetians and Genoese. The war began with revolutions in nearly all the
towns west of Constantinople up to and including
Thessalonica, in which the governing classes were overthrown by radical regimes. John VI Kantakouzenos
entered Constantinople in triumph in 1347 and married
John V to his daughter. Before long, the young emperor
was persuaded to turn against his father-in-law. Another
civil war ensued, which ended with Kantakouzenos'
abdication in 1354 and retirement to the court of his son
Manuel in the Peloponnese.

The real victors by these civil wars were the foreign
rivals of Byzantium: the Genoese, who helped themselves
to several islands, the Serbs and the Turks. The kingdom
of Serbia had been a great power since the exploitation of
important silver mines in the late 13th century had made
King Stephen Milutin (1282–1321) the richest monarch in
the Balkans. Milutin's grandson Stephen Dušan conquered
almost the whole Balkan area; during the Byzantine civil
war of 1341–47 he occupied Thessaly, Epirus and all
Macedonia outside Thessalonica. In 1345 he proclaimed
himself emperor, and might have made his claim good at
Byzantine expense had he not died in 1355.

The future lay with the Turks, and especially with the
state which Osman (who gave his name to the Osmanli or
Ottoman dynasty) had created out of the Byzantine
province of Bithynia. In 1346 John Kantakouzenos gained
the upper hand in the civil war by allying with Osman's
son Orhan, who received his daughter in marriage and
supplied him with troops. This encouraged the Osmanlis
to advance into Europe; they acquired a bridgehead in
1354 when an earthquake shattered the walls of Gallipoli.

The emperor John V, senior emperor 1355–91, did
what he could to remedy the situation, but the civil war
had left the empire completely devoid of material resources. Even the promise of Church union and a begging
journey by the emperor to the west did not bring military
help from the Latin powers. At the same time, John had to
cope with opposition from his own family: his sons
Manuel II and Andronikos IV and his grandson John VII
all wanted an imperial title and lands which they could call
their own. Only Manuel put the interests of the empire
first; the others were willing to intrigue with any foreign
power in order to further their interests. The Osmanlis had
little difficulty in conquering Thrace and Macedonia. In
1369 Sultan Murad I established his capital in Adrianople.
In 1371 he wiped out a Serbian army at the battle of the
Maritsa river. Manuel II for a short time resisted from
Thessalonica, but in 1387 he was forced to abandon the
city. Murad's son Bayezid I received the submission of
mainland Greece and conquered Bulgaria.

The empire was now reduced to Constantinople itself and Manuel II (1391–1425) began his reign as a Turkish vassal. The Turkish danger was now causing alarm in the west, and some efforts were made to relieve Constantinople. Manuel set out for Italy, France and England, but failed to enlist any real support. Constantinople might have fallen during his absence had not Bayezid and his army been annihilated in 1402 by the Mongol conqueror Timur (Tamerlane). This allowed the empire a breathing space in which it briefly regained Thessalonica. However, with the accession of Murad II in 1421, the Osmanlis again turned to the attack. Manuel's son John VIII in desperation reopened negotiations with the pope; these led to the Council of Florence (1439), which the emperor attended and which brought the Byzantine Church under papal jurisdiction. But like the union of 1274, this was bitterly opposed by the Orthodox, and soon became a dead letter.

The final struggle between Byzantium and the Turks occurred under a new emperor, John VIII's brother Constantine XI (1449–53), and a new sultan, Mehmet II (1451–81). The siege began in April 1453. Constantine put up a gallant defense, but the Turks had numerical superiority and a technological advantage in the cannon which they had acquired from the west. On 29 May the besiegers stormed the walls. The emperor was killed, the city was sacked and Mehmet entered his new capital in triumph.

Not until 1460 did Mehmet expel the Palaiologoi from the city of Mistra near Sparta. Imperial decentralization and bad communications had transformed the Byzantine province in the Peloponnese into an independent exarchate which, from the 1370s, had expanded at the expense of the Latin rulers of the peninsula, and had made the court at Mistra more brilliant than that of Constantinople. The empire of the Palaiologoi was survived by about a year by the state which a branch of the Komnenos family had founded in 1204 at the eastern end of the Black Sea, and which their descendants insisted on calling an empire, in defiance of Constantinople. The capital, Trebizond, fell in 1461.

The final age of Byzantium, although it saw the collapse of the empire, was a period of general prosperity reflected in the rich and elaborate monuments of the empire and its rival principalities. Outside the capital, the most remarkable remains are certainly those of Mistra, capital of the Byzantine domains in the Peloponnese, where a whole city is still virtually preserved, with several churches decorated with frescoes, and a substantial palace, as well as the streets. Two churches of Thessalonica, St Catherine and the Holy Apostles, date from the Palaiologan period, as do the churches in Mesembria (Nessebar, in Bulgaria) and the monasteries of the Meteora, perched on high and steep rocks. In the other states, the church of the Paregoritissa in Arta in Epirus and that of St Sophia in Trebizond are worthy of consideration among the finest monuments of the time. The period also saw a great

The monasteries of the Meteora in northern Greece. *Above:* the steep rocks, surmounted by monasteries, tower above the town of Stagoi. This town was the seat of a bishop from the 9th century, but was probably never much larger than it appears in this sketch of 1744. *Top:* a modern view of the monastery of Roussanou, a hermitage founded in 1388 and turned into a monastery in 1639.

development of painting in which a more lifelike style was developed, as is evident in the frescoes of the capital and Mistra.

Byzantine society. Byzantium was racially an extremely diverse society. The invasions and migrations of late antiquity reduced the native peoples of the Balkans and Asia Minor, and added Germanic, Celtic, Slavic and Hunnic elements to the army and the rural population, while the towns received a constant influx of immigrants from North Africa, Italy, Egypt, Palestine, Syria and Armenia. Throughout the Middle Ages several waves of invaders from Central Asia entered the European territories of the empire, while the coasts and the eastern frontier were open to the Arabs and later the Turks. From the 11th century there was a movement of western Europeans to the Levant, as crusaders, merchants and mercenaries. To appreciate this ethnic diversity, one only has to consider the origin of some late Byzantine aristocratic names: Tornikes (Armenian); Asan (Cuman); Raoul

(French); Melikes (Turkish).

Two elements call for special comment, the Slavs and the Armenians. Not only did the Slavs colonize the whole Balkan peninsula in the 6th and 7th centuries, but also large numbers of them were forcibly transferred to Asia Minor by certain emperors. The Armenian homeland was the mountain area of the Caucasus, but by natural or forced migration and by service in the army, the Armenians came to settle in all parts of Asia Minor, and to be represented in all walks of life. No other group provided the empire with so many talented soldiers and administrators.

The Byzantines took little account of a man's racial origin, so long as he professed to be an Orthodox Christian and a loyal subject of the "Roman" emperor in Constantinople. In practice, too, he had to be fluent in Greek, which from the 7th century was the only official language.

The Roman, Christian and Greek heritage in Byzantine civilization was heavily invested in the city of Constantinople. With its large dimensions, its ordered layout of avenues, colonnades and *fora* with triumphal columns and imperial statues, its baths, Hippodrome and cisterns, Constantinople was the most imposing Christian city of the early and high Middle Ages. The old Rome was still a metropolitan center, thanks to the great prestige of its apostolic tradition, but the papal curia was hardly the equivalent of the vast imperial court which aspired to the political domination of the world and absorbed the revenues of a subcontinent. The ceremonial, personnel and expenditure of the imperial regime accounted for the lives of a city population which, before 1204 at least, numbered several hundreds of thousands.

Many cities could boast an older Christian tradition than Constantinople, but few could show so many visible signs of holiness. The sources reveal the names of some 500 churches which were founded within its walls during the period of Christian domination. Besides these, Constantinople possessed the largest collection of Christian relics that was to be found anywhere. Most of these relics were kept in the chapel of the imperial palace; they had been collected by generations of emperors with a ruthlessness equal to that of modern art collectors. A holy relic was the supernatural protector, the *genius loci*, of the place where it was kept, and in building up such a huge collection the emperors not only wanted to improve their capital but to diminish the prestige of all other centers.

It is unlikely that the Byzantine rulers, apart from rare individuals like Leo VI and Constantine VII, made similar efforts to collect works of ancient Greek literature. Even in late antiquity, a Classical education at Constantinople was probably less thorough than that which was to be had at Athens, Antioch or Alexandria. But Constantinople survived until 1204 with its libraries unsacked: all the texts which form the basis of Greek studies today have come down to us in manuscript traditions which at some stage passed through medieval Constantinople, mainly the

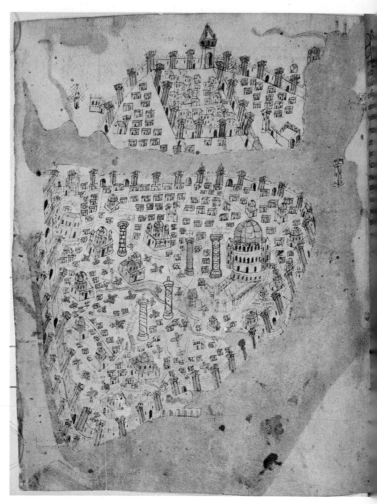

Map of Constantinople illustrating Cristoforo Buondelmonti's *Book of the Archipelago*. The representations of buildings are fairly fanciful. British Library, MS Cotton Vespasian A XIII, c. 1422.

libraries of the palace and patriarchate. The copying of ancient texts went on throughout the Byzantine period and testifies to a constant, if limited, demand. Byzantine intellectuals adopted ancient Greek as a mandarin language, with regrettable results both for it and for them, but in so doing they were perpetuating a tradition which had existed since the 3rd century BC, and which would have died without them.

The city of Constantinople. Throughout its history as a Christian city, Constantinople lived within a framework which had been established in the 4th, 5th and 6th centuries. The perimeter fixed by Theodosius II in the early 5th century proved more than ample for future expansion. Emperors built themselves summer palaces outside the walls, and the Genoese had their own fortified colony of Galata (Pera) across the Golden Horn; otherwise, the old city accommodated both the ghetto life of the foreign minorities and the "suburban" privacy of the rich. The architectural setting of public life was as it had been at the end of the 6th century: the defenses, public

Niketas Choniates, historian of the period 1118–1206: miniature portrait from a 14th-century manuscript of his work. National Library, Vienna, Hist. Gr. 13.

cover the streets with their buildings, leaving filth and shadows to the poor and the foreigners. There murders are carried out, and robberies, and all other crimes which delight in darkness. Since life is lived without justice in this city, which has almost as many masters as it has wealthy men, and nearly as many thieves as it has paupers, here the criminal has neither fear nor shame, where the crime goes unavenged by the law and does not appear in the open daylight. In all things it exceeds the norm, for just as it vanquishes other cities by its riches, so too by its vices.''

Two centuries later, after the depopulation and dilapidation caused by the Latin occupation, the scale of Constantinople did not impress foreigners: an Arab geographer wrote, "In the interior of the town are plowed fields, gardens and many houses in ruins," and a western observer remarked that "hardly the third part of the city is inhabited; the rest is gardens or fields, or vineyards, or waste ground." The imperial court and the public worship of St Sophia continued to function until the end, but the games at the Hippodrome, which had been the main occasions when the emperor appeared before his people, had ceased after 1204, and only the occasional joust took place there.

The only important secular buildings erected in the capital by emperors in the Dark Ages and later were palaces, and for these, at least, no expense was spared. Justinian II, Theophilos, Basil I, Constantine VII, Nikephoros II and Manuel I all made additions and alterations to the great palace near the Hippodrome. Of the numerous imperial residences in other parts of the city, two are worth mentioning here: the Mangana palace below the ancient acropolis of Byzantium, built in the 9th century, and the complex in the Blachernae quarter at the northern end of the land walls, near the church which contained a precious veil of the Virgin. This palace was developed in the 11th and 12th centuries, especially by the Komnenoi, and after 1261 it became the main residence of the Palaiologan emperors. This "flight to the suburbs" was symptomatic of the fact that the imperial dynasty was now only one aristocratic family among many. One chronicler states that the relatives and followers of Alexios I "built houses which by their dimensions seemed to be cities, and in magnificence were not inferior to the royal palaces."

Of all these structures practically nothing has survived. The ruined Tekfur Saray near the land walls is probably to be identified with the palace built by Constantine Palaiologos, son of Michael VIII. At Maltepe, on the Asiatic side of the Bosphorus, a large Byzantine substructure has been discovered and identified as the palace of Bryas which the emperor Theophilos built according to an Arabic model.

In conformity with their 5th- and 6th-century predecessors, the Byzantine emperors of the post-iconoclastic period were great church builders. Their foundations were monasteries and chapels for restricted use, rather than places of public worship. The architectural type was some

amenities, streets and squares, Hippodrome and St Sophia, were all the work of emperors who ruled before the period discussed in this chapter. The middle and late Byzantine periods saw many major constructions, but these were not intended to beautify the city as a whole or to serve it as a community.

The extent to which civic life had declined by the 12th century is apparent from the description left by a French visitor to the court of Manuel I, Odo of Deuil. After describing the palace of Blachernae (see below), Odo writes: "The third side of the triangle of the city has fields, but it is fortified by a double wall with towers, which stretches from the sea almost two miles to the palace. This [wall] is not robust, nor does it raise its towers to any great height, but the city, as I judge, trusts in its populousness and in the long peace which it has enjoyed. Inside the walls the land is empty; it is under the plow and hoe, having gardens which provide all manner of vegetables. Subterranean aqueducts enter from the outside, which lavishly distribute fresh water to the city. This is dirty and foul, and in many places damned in perpetual darkness, for the rich

variant of the domed cross-in-square (see Visual Story 4), whose style was set by the church of the Virgin of the Pharos, which Michael III constructed as the palace chapel. Another palace church was the Nea Ekklesia, built by Basil I, who also restored the church of the Holy Apostles, the traditional imperial mausoleum, and built others in and outside the city. None of these structures remains, although the five-domed plan of the Nea was followed in the monastery church which a government official, Constantine Lips, built in the reign of Leo VI and survives, badly damaged, as the more northerly in the complex known as the Fener-i-Isa Cami. From the reign of Romanos Lekapenos we have the church of the Myrelaion monastery. Of the churches which the prodigal emperors of the mid-11th century built in and around Constantinople nothing survives, although the monastery church of Nea Moni on the island of Chios, founded by Constantine IX Monomachos in 1045, gives some idea of what these may have been like. Rather more churches are left from the period of the Komnenoi, most of them founded by the ruling dynasty. The core of the Kariye Cami was probably the work of Alexios I's youngest son Isaac. The Eski Imaret Cami near the Golden Horn is identified with the monastery of Christ Pantepoptes, founded c. 1100 by Alexios' mother Anna Dalassena. The monastery of Christ Pantokrator was founded by John II and his wife Irene. Its three churches (Zeyrek Kilise Cami),

of which the central one was used as a dynastic mausoleum, form the finest architectural ensemble of the Komnenian period.

None of the surviving church buildings in Istanbul is an integral structure of the Palaiologan period, although some new foundations are known to have been made, and there are several standing examples of churches which were taken over and restored by prominent members of the early Palaiologan court. Michael VIII's wife Theodora built a new church to the south of that of Constantine Lips and surrounded it on two sides with an ambulatory. Both the main church and the ambulatory are full of *arcisolia* (recesses) marking the tombs of members of the family. Similar phenomena can be observed in the churches which contain the most famous mosaic decoration of the period, the Chora (Kariye Cami) and the Virgin Pammakaristos (Fethiye Cami). Here the Palaiologan additions to the 12th-century structures serve as funerary chapels, containing tombs which record in portrait and inscription the names of the deceased, all relatives of the restorers: Theodore Metochites, Andronikos II's minister, and Michael Glabas Tarchaneiotes, a military official. These constructions testify to the extent to which religious patronage at the time was linked with aristocratic family pride.

Decline of the provincial town. Constantinople's continuity of existence ensured that Byzantine society never lacked an urban culture. Yet this culture seems to have been maintained at the expense of urban life almost everywhere else throughout the empire. Only one other city succeeded in retaining the shape and dimensions of an ancient metropolis: Thessalonica, the second city of the empire. The sources imply by their silence, and archaeological evidence confirms, that most Byzantine provincial towns, even where they occupied the sites of large ancient cities, were built on a very lowly scale. Rubble was

Left: the Tekfur Saray, near the land walls of Constantinople, called the palace of Constantine Porphyrogenitos. The reference is probably to a son of Michael VIII rather than to the 10th-century emperor.

Opposite: the Kariye Cami in Constantinople, the core of which was probably the work of Alexios I's youngest son Isaac.

Below: the substructure of the palace built by the Emperor Theophilos at Bryas (Maltepe) near Constantinople.

the most common building material. Houses were mostly of one story; there was no orderly street plan. Where the walls of the late Roman city could be held, as at Nicaea and Philadelphia, the settlement might occupy a wide area – but with no more density than in Constantinople. Otherwise, it was generally restricted to the cramped space of a fortified citadel. There seem to have been practically no buildings other than houses, fortifications and churches.

The explanation for this decline of the provincial town is not hard to find. The invasions of the Dark Ages destroyed and depopulated the Roman cities, and when the provinces were reoccupied the need was primarily for fortified bases from which to resist; there was little room for culture or for economic activity beyond the provisioning of the army. The word popularly used to denote a town, even Constantinople, was not *polis* but *kastron*, a Hellenization of the Latin word which gives us the word "castle." The provincial aristocracy was a warrior class with heroic values and a stern, Old Testament morality. Provincials with other inclinations had to follow them in the capital, and once established there, they and their descendants had no incentive to leave. Any comfort which the 12th-century churchman Michael Choniates may have derived from the fact that his provincial see lay in the historic city of Athens could not survive contact with the barbarous Athenians of his day, although he was quick to

perceive that their wretchedness was caused largely by Constantinopolitan rapacity. This being the case, it needed more than conditions of peace for the provincial towns to flourish: it needed the temporary fall of Constantinople into foreign hands and the permanent weakening of the central government. The cities of western Asia Minor enjoyed a new lease of life during the period of the empire of Nicaea. The impressive late Byzantine monuments of Arta, Mistra and Trebizond owe their existence, and their cosmopolitan flavor, to the fact that these towns were political centers independent of Constantinople.

Commerce clearly played some part in a town's prosperity: besides Constantinople and Thessalonica, great ports with extensive manufactures, there was the silk industry of Thebes, the fur trade of Kastoria and the wine trade of Monemvasia. The government realized the importance of commerce for state revenue and did what it could to protect its own merchants, until the 11th century at least. There were not the same strictures against usury as in Latin Christendom, and wealth could purchase the attributes of social status. The ruling elite of 14th-century Ioannina, which numbered some very noble families, engaged in trade. Yet the prevailing ethos in Byzantium, as in most monarchies, discouraged professional commercialism. Since Byzantine commercial interests could not, as in the more loosely organized world of western

Europe, take advantage of power struggles between the recognized orders of society – the monarchy, the aristocracy and the Church – in order to emancipate themselves, they were forced to yield to foreign competition.

Thus outside the milieu of Constantinople, and supporting the dominant administrative superstructure, the empire was a rural society, "medieval" in the most popular sense of the term: a society where men were classed into those who fought, those who prayed and those who tilled the soil. During the 7th, 8th and 9th centuries there may have been some confusion between the first and the third of these categories, but otherwise there was no doubt that the peasantry existed in order to enable the other orders to serve God and their ruler with the minimum of mundane concern. Continuity of Roman law, Greek learning and a money economy gave the Byzantines a sophistication which was ultimately deceptive, because it denied them the potentially more rewarding experience of discovering these traditions anew.

Left: the citadel of Monemvasia on the east coast of the Peloponnese. The town was famous for its wine trade (malmsey in English): terraces of empty vineyards can be seen on the mainland.

Below: the palace at Mistra, the capital of the Palaiologoi in the Peloponnese. The main building is 15th century.

The Defenses of the Empire

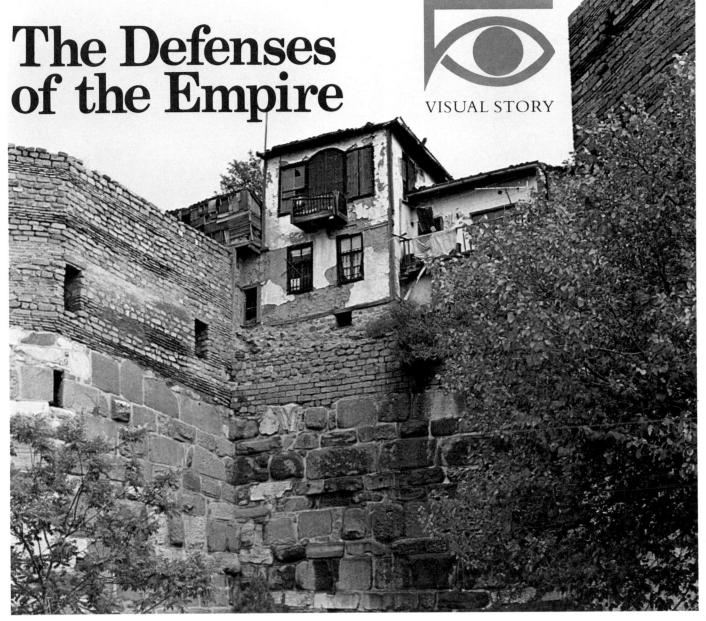

After the loss of the west, the eastern provinces successfully defended themselves for three centuries with fortifications, troops and diplomacy. But ultimately they were unable to resist the onslaughts of the early 7th century when Avars and Slavs overran the Balkans, and the Persians, seizing the eastern provinces, left Asia Minor in ruins. Although these were defeated by the heroic efforts of Heraclius, a new and more determined enemy appeared in the Arabs who permanently removed Syria, Palestine and Egypt from imperial control. In this supreme crisis of the empire's existence, new systems of defense had to be evolved; their efficacy enabled the Byzantine state to survive and ultimately to move on the offensive.

The social and economic structure of Asia Minor had been ruined by the long war with the Persians which left cities and countryside devastated. In its place the Byzantines created an administrative system in which large districts called "themes" replaced the provinces. Each theme was governed by a *strategos* or general who commanded the troops of the whole district and to whom the civil government came to be subordinated. The system was simple and efficient. The headquarters of the three original army themes into which Asia Minor was divided were powerfully fortified cities on major highways. *Above*, the walls of Ancyra (Ankara), a thematic capital and from the 8th century headquarters of an army of 8,000 men.

The strength of the empire and its ability to resist the most persistent enemy resided in its centralized organization, its well-trained and equipped army and navy, its advanced technology and its powerful defensive works.

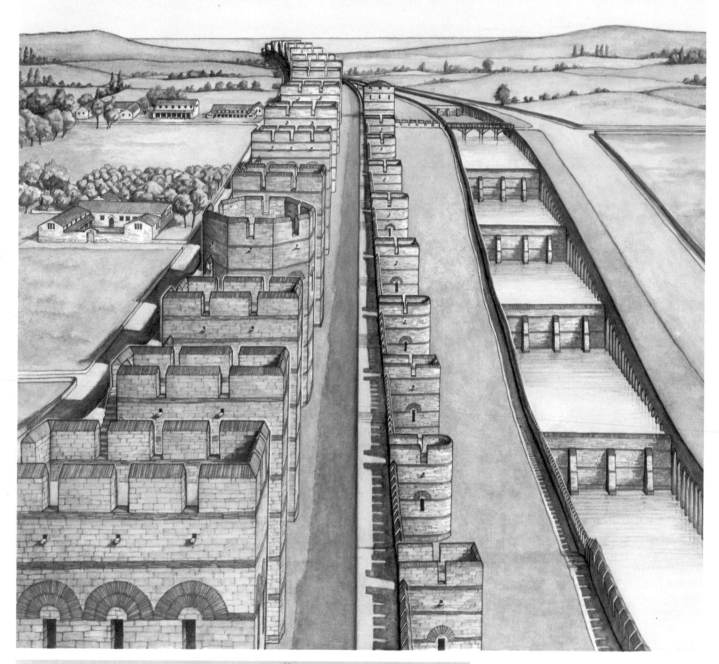

The walls of Constantinople. The original walls of Constantine were replaced in the time of Theodosius II to embrace a larger area and to meet the threat of Attila the Hun. The fortifications, the most advanced of their day, consisted of a ditch 60 feet wide and 20 deep, an outer wall 15 feet high behind which troops could assemble, and the main rampart whose walls, 15 feet thick and 40 feet high, were protected by towers. The rampart was so powerful that it held until breached by the cannons of the Turks in 1453. Reconstruction after Krischen.

Above and right: the steep and inaccessible acropolis of Sardis illustrates the fate of many cities in the epoch of the invasions. In late antiquity Sardis was a busy provincial capital extending far into the plain. After its destruction by the Persians in 616, the city retreated to the hilltop and was surrounded by heavy walls built from the ruins of its ancient buildings. Some of the inhabitants lived in the citadel, going forth by day to tend their flocks and fields; others occupied settlements resembling villages scattered over the ancient site, one of them at the ruined temple of Artemis – whose columns are visible in the middle distance (*above*).

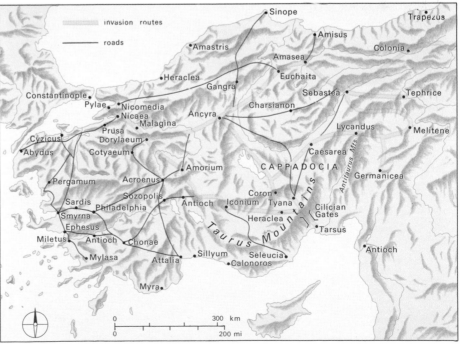

Below right: Asia Minor during the Arab attacks. The Arab attacks consisted of major expeditions by land or sea, usually with the capital as their goal, and the annual raids which were primarily for booty. Most attacks by land came through the Cilician Gates to the Anatolian plateau, where the raiders would scatter in different directions, to return home after devastating and robbing the country. The thematic forces could be easily mobilized against raiders, and, in case of a major enemy expedition, news could be sent rapidly to the capital by a series of beacon fires on mountain tops between the Cilician Gates and the Sea of Marmora. The imperial forces could then set out across Anatolia, receiving the thematic contingents at appointed places.

The harbor of Attalia (Antalya), *above* in an engraving of 1840, *left* as seen today. The enemy came by sea as well as land, coasting along the southern shore of Asia Minor on plundering raids or major expeditions. The Arab fleet made great advances, twice reaching the capital and laying siege to it in 663 and 716. The naval theme of the Cibyrrhaeots, organized to meet this threat, had its headquarters at Attalia, the only place on the southern coast which survived as a major city. The city was a base for raw materials and supplies for the fleet, for the construction of ships, and for the thematic navy which would set out from this harbor to intercept attack or make raids on the Arabs. City and harbor were surrounded by massive walls, rebuilt in the early 10th century.

Hidden defenses: an underground city of Cappadocia. Under attack by the Arabs, the inhabitants excavated several such refuges into the soft rock. These cities reached a depth of eight or ten floors, with rooms for dwelling, storage and worship arranged along tunnels like streets (*right*). *Top*: a reconstruction (after Akok) of a part of one of these complexes, with an individual suite of rooms on the right. *Above*: large millstones were rolled sideways to block the entrances.

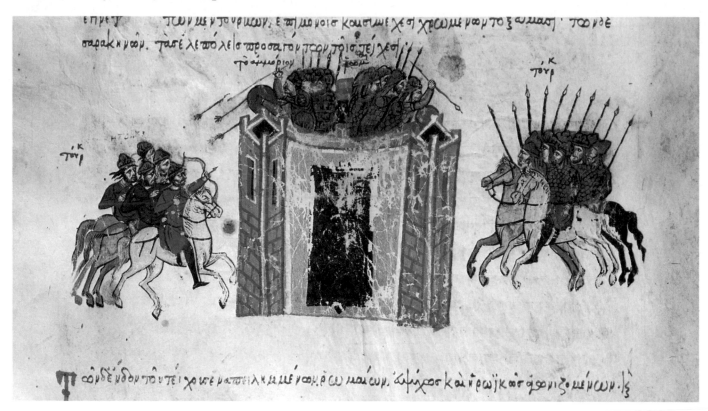

Above: attack by land: the siege of Amorium by the Arabs in 838. In this 13th-century manuscript illustration the Arabs are anachronistically labeled Turks. In the center, a tower symbolizing the city is defended by the thematic troops. The Saracen forces are shown both as light-armed archers and heavy-armed cavalry.

Below: attack by sea: the capture of Thessalonica in 904 by the Christian renegade, Leo of Attalia. The illustration shows Arab troops wearing turbans slaughtering the inhabitants of the city, represented by walls and an arcade. In the center, the Arabs bring their captives to the fleet waiting in the harbor.

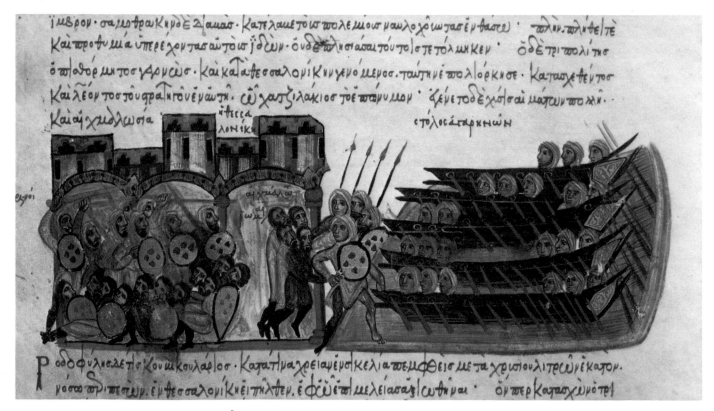

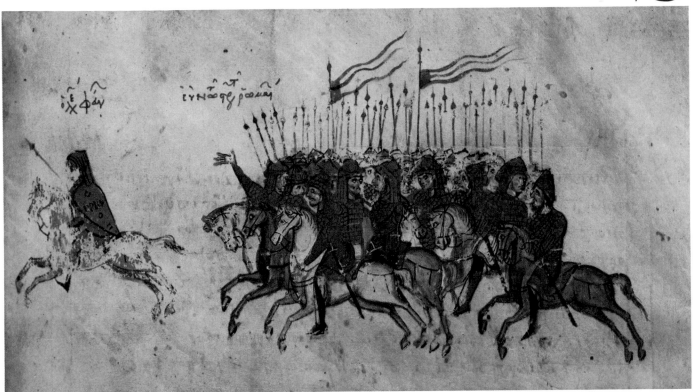

Above: the Byzantine army. A division of heavy-armed troops, all cavalry, follows its leader. The thematic armies, the backbone of imperial defense, were generally of this type – mounted warriors wearing armor and metal helmets, armed with swords and lances. This highly mobile force was supplemented with infantry and light-armed troops.

Below: the secret weapon: Greek fire, invented in the 7th century, was a liquid which apparently contained saltpeter, sulfur and oil. It was propelled from long tubes mounted on special fire ships and could not easily be extinguished with water. Greek fire was an important element in Byzantine victories at sea. National Library, Madrid.

Warrior saints. In addition to its walls and weapons, the empire relied heavily on supernatural aid. Valued relics and patron saints worked miracles which could and did save many cities from the assaults of the enemy. Some saints, often of obscure origin, became famed as warriors whose patronage was especially effective for defense. The most famous were St George of Lydda in Palestine, St Theodore of Euchaeta in northern Anatolia and St Demetrius of Thessalonica, who saved his city from the Avars and Slavs on many occasions. *Above* we see St Theodore Stratelates and *below* St Theodore Tiro, both frescoes from the nave of the Church of the Protaton on Mount Athos painted by Manuel Panselinos (late 13th or early 14th century).

5.The Church and the Arts

The role of religion. In order to appreciate the monuments of Byzantine civilization which can be seen today, it is important to have some understanding of Byzantine religion. This is best approached by way of the more familiar Christian traditions of the west. Like medieval England, Byzantium was a society where the supernatural, in the form of a closely defined Christian God, was consciously given full priority; where demons, witches and miracles were adduced to explain even the most rational phenomena; and where modern romantics have looked for the beauty of holiness. It is no accident that in the Balkans and Asia Minor, as throughout western Europe, the type of medieval building most frequently encountered is the church.

The Byzantine Church, which gave rise to the Eastern Orthodox Churches of today, and the Latin Church, the ancestor of both the Roman Catholic and Protestant Churches, were both based on a theological and hierarchical tradition which had taken seven centuries to produce. By the 9th century, when the first serious quarrel between Rome and Constantinople occurred, the most explosive doctrinal issues had been resolved by seven ecumenical councils, the authority of whose decrees was unchallenged both in east and west. The earliest councils had dealt with the Arian heresy which had threatened to destroy the concept of the Trinity. Nearly all the councils which followed, in the 5th, 6th and 7th centuries, were concerned with defining Christ: the idea that he was one person but of two natures, human and divine, was never accepted without serious qualification by most people in the easternmost provinces of the Roman Empire; indeed, the Christological dispute was not properly settled until the largely Monophysite populations of Egypt and Syria came under Islam – a faith which was both more tolerant of their differences and more sympathetic to their distrust of the Incarnation. After the seventh and last council to be recognized in east and west, the second Council of Nicaea (787) which restored icon-worship, the Church appeared to have dealt with all major threats to uniformity and stability. Ecclesiastical authority now resided in two cities instead of five, for with the fall of Alexandria, Antioch and Jerusalem to the Arabs, these patriarchates could not provide the same leadership as those of the old imperial capitals, Rome and Constantinople. Christian civilization now belonged exclusively to the Greco-Roman tradition, in language, in learning and in its unqualified devotion to an incarnate God. Henceforth any doctrine which smacked of extreme Monophysitism or Dualism was severely punished both in the Latin west and in the Greek east.

At the same time, however, the Churches of Rome and Constantinople had developed profound differences which, in the 9th century, and again in the 10th, led to estrangement and schism. Latin had fallen out of use in the

Previous page: a priest holding a 16th-century icon at the monastery of St Neophytos in the mountains of southern Cyprus.

A perfectly preserved 12th-century Christ Pantokrator in the dome of the church of Panagia tou Arakou, Lagoudera Monastery, Cyprus.

east and Greek in the west, which meant that western and eastern Christians did not read the same Church Fathers or use the same theological vocabulary. Already by the 9th century the visible differences were such as to inflame the prejudices of the uneducated: the Latins used unleavened and the Greeks leavened bread in the Eucharist; different rules of fasting were observed; Byzantine priests wore long beards while Latin clerics were clean-shaven. Such differences were not, however, legitimate causes for schism. When Byzantine and Latin theologians anathematized each other, they did so because the Latins had added to the part of the Creed dealing with the Holy Spirit a formula to the effect that the third person of the Trinity proceeds "from the Son" (*Filioque*) as well as from the Father. The Byzantines claimed that this addition was unjustified since it was not sanctioned by what they considered to be an ecumenical council; in any case, it diminished the monarchy of God the Father. The Latins claimed that the addition was necessary in order to explain the operation of the Spirit, and to leave no doubt as to the importance of the Son – the formula had originally been introduced by missionaries combating the Arian heresy among the Visigoths of Spain. In the 9th century, and again in the controversies surrounding the stillborn reconciliations of Lyons (1274) and Florence (1439), volumes were written in condemnation, justification or modification of the *Filioque*. For the medieval mind, the discrepancy was a vital one, and some modern Orthodox hold that it fully expresses the differences in outlook between eastern and western Christians. Be that as it may, the *Filioque* issue does not adequately explain or define what the Byzantines felt to be special about their form of Christianity.

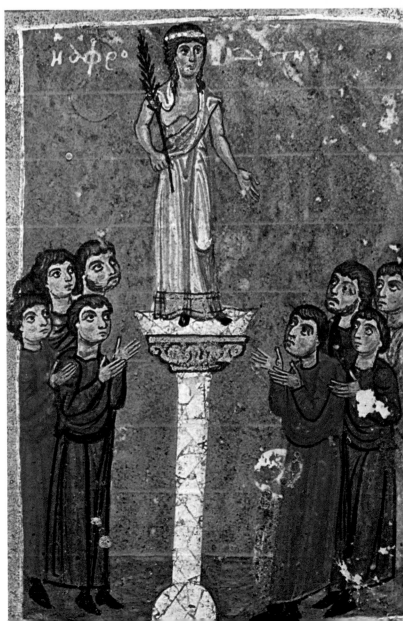

Above: a miniature icon of Basil the Great on an icon stand from a 13th-century Athos manuscript of the liturgy, Dionysiou 105.

Above right: the Church in council. A 15th-century fresco in the church of St Sozomenos, Galata, Cyprus, depicting the third ecumenical council held at Ephesus in 431 AD.

Below right: pagan adoration of Aphrodite, from a 12th-century Athos manuscript (Panteleimon 6) of the homilies of St Gregory of Nazianzen. Byzantine artists commonly depicted pagan idols standing on top of columns, inspired no doubt by the many examples of ancient statuary to be seen in Constantinople.

Organization of the Church. Perhaps the most important single fact about the Byzantine Church is that it developed within the framework of a powerful, authoritarian monarchy, to which it was organically integrated at all levels. At Church councils and synods emperors presided. The patriarchal cathedral of Constantinople was also the greatest monument to imperial munificence: Constantine's and Justinian's church of the Holy Wisdom, Hagia Sophia. The Church functioned as a department of state. At the head of it was the establishment presided over by the patriarch and known collectively as the Great Church. It included many priests with liturgical functions and a large bureaucratic staff concerned with Church property, canon law, ecclesiastical appointments and relations with Churches outside the political sphere of the empire. The ecclesiastical diocese of Constantinople was divided into provinces, each administered by a metropolitan having under him subordinate bishops in every town – indeed, whatever the size of the settlement, it was the presence of the bishop which gave it "municipal" status in Byzantine eyes. In addition, there were archbishops who theoretically had no provinces, although two late Byzantine archbishoprics, those of Ochrid and Cyprus, became the most important sees under Constantinople. At times when the Slav rulers of Bulgaria, Russia and Serbia claimed imperial status, the ecclesiastical leaders of these countries were recognized as patriarchs; otherwise they were known as archbishops. Bishops were served by a staff of episcopal clergy and parish priests. In principle, prelates above the rank of bishop did not adjudicate alone: local matters were handled by the provincial synod of the metropolitan, and major questions were referred to the synod of Constantinople, which included all the metropolitans and bishops who happened to be in the capital. In practice, the patriarch had an overriding vote, and he in turn was at the mercy of the emperor.

In political terms, therefore, the Church was subordinate to the state. This statement does not, however, properly reflect the position of the Church in Byzantine society or in the Byzantine mind. For the Orthodox believer, the Church was the whole communion of the faithful existing in eternity. The monarch in this polity was Christ himself, addressed in prayer by the very titles, *despotes* (absolute master) and *basileus* (king), which belonged to the earthly ruler. The court of heaven was composed of the Holy Family, apostles, evangelists, martyrs and Church Fathers; it had an army led by the angelic host, with St Michael at its head, and numbering saintly mortals whose cults enjoyed immense prestige in the middle and late Byzantine periods: Sts George, Demetrios, Theodore Tyro and Theodore Stratelates. Of this monarchy, that on earth was only a very transitory viceroyalty, which would lose its strength and its *raison d'être* if it departed from the divine original. Human nature being what it was, the chances of losing touch with heaven were infinite; the lines could only be kept open by men whose professions did not automatically lead to worldliness and sin.

The Byzantines did not share the Augustinian tradition of the early western Middle Ages, which held that all political power was inherently evil. However, they believed that no good would come of it if the emperor was not a good Christian, which meant being Orthodox in doctrine, pure in morals, merciful to his people, generous to his clergy and humble in spirit towards his spiritual confessor. The emperor who used his power to defy these

The Trinity, surrounded by the Heavenly Host. An 11th-century miniature from the National Library, Vienna, Suppl. gr. 52.

ideals was no better than a pagan persecutor. All emperors could push through controversial legislation by appointing compliant patriarchs and bishops, but the reactions aroused by those who went this far – Leo III and Constantine V with their iconoclasm; Constantine VI with his "adulterous" second marriage; Leo VI with his fourth marriage; Alexios I with his emergency requisitioning of Church valuables; Michael VIII with his Church union – were powerful deterrents. The emperor's standing depended very much on the empire's political fortunes. In the last declining centuries of Byzantium, the spiritual authority of the patriarch commanded much greater respect than the political authority of the emperor, both in the Byzantine "commonwealth" of Slav nations, and at home, where patriarchal anointment came to play a major part as one of the ceremonies which marked an emperor's elevation to the throne.

Education and philanthropy. The ambiguity of the power relationship between the Byzantine emperor and his clergy naturally gives rise to the assumption that Church and state were less distinct in Byzantium than in the medieval west. It is true that the Byzantines never formulated a "sun and moon" doctrine of two separate orders, spiritual and temporal, such as that which grew out of the power struggle between the medieval papacy and the German Empire. It is equally true that its existence within the structure of a mature state, and within the walls of an almost impregnable metropolitan city, made the men seeking the wisdom of God put behind them in their teens. The schools of the monasteries and the patriarchate dealt in theology – the rich and philosophical theology of the Greek Fathers – which was called the "inner learning" as opposed to the "outer learning" of rhetoric, mathematics and logic. Thus there were always two self-sufficient and distinct educational traditions.

Much has been made of the philanthropy and social welfare provided by the Byzantine Church, and indeed it seems that the orphanages, old-age homes and hospitals of Constantinople were run by monks. However, almsgiving, philanthropy and benefaction were ideal imperial as well as Christian attributes, and the initiative in founding charitable institutions seems to have come more often from emperors than from churchmen. As in every other type of patronage, the name of Justinian is foremost; of others we may mention in particular John II Komnenos, whose monastery of Christ Pantokrator administered a large hospital, with 50 beds and as many doctors.

As in the west, the provincial administration of the Church was more stable and permanent than that of the state, and when the processes of secular government failed, the bishop frequently emerged as leader of the local population. Yet Byzantine bishops never became feudal lords, ruling like princes and behaving like warriors, in the manner of many western medieval prelates. The idea of the holy war was not alien to Byzantium, a society which spent its entire existence fighting against the eastern infidel, but that of the crusade was. The Byzantines could not feel the western impulse to go and conquer the holy places, partly because they did not have the excess population to spare for distant military adventures unrelated to their own defense needs; partly because Jerusalem, Nazareth and Bethlehem did not mean to them what they meant to northern Europeans, for whom the pilgrimage had become the main point of contact with the relics of Christian antiquity. By 1204 Constantinople was, as we remarked in the last chapter, the greatest repository of Christian museum pieces anywhere in the world. When the Latins conquered the city, these were the principal objects of their greed. An English priest in 1206 stole a piece of the True Cross from the imperial chapel, and when, on his return home, he repented of the theft, the relic passed into the possession of the obscure Cluniac priory of Bromholm on the Norfolk coast. Within a generation this had become one of the most prosperous pilgrimage centers in England. This allows us to appreciate what effect the concentration of so many such relics in Constantinople was likely to produce on the Byzantine mind: the new Jerusalem, like the new Rome, must have seemed far more impressive than the old.

The Byzantine, therefore, grew up in a society where the physical sources of holiness were very immediate and familiar, and although he might feel that his earthly environment was out of harmony with heaven, he could glimpse the latter in his splendid churches, and did not

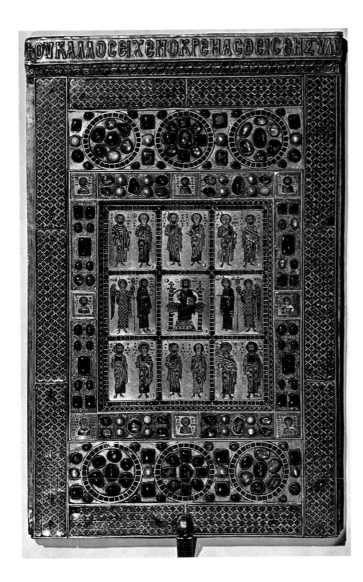

Reliquary case, commissioned by the Emperor Constantine Porphyrogenitos, designed to contain a relic of the True Cross. Cathedral Treasury, Limburg-an-der-Lahn.

Byzantine Church less ready to take on secular attributes than was the case in the west. The Roman papacy had to conduct diplomatic business which in Constantinople was left to the imperial administration; thus it took on the character of an earthly monarchy. In the west the Church preserved all that was left of Roman civilization in a barbarous society, and therefore felt a responsibility for the spread of education and law. In Byzantium there were (except perhaps in the 7th and 8th centuries) elementary schools and private academies, and there existed, on and off, state-sponsored facilities for the training of imperial functionaries. As we have seen, highbrow literature was available and had a snob-value, so that Byzantine churchmen could not feel any responsibility to civilize laymen, except perhaps in the Slav lands that were converted from paganism; indeed, ancient Greek literature and philosophy were counted worldly and childish things, which need to see it through the eyes of others. The priesthood never altogether became a caste which acted as sole intermediary between the human and the divine. The Byzantine layman was encouraged to feel that he could participate in all aspects of worship beyond the administration of the sacraments. A hostile western observer of the 14th century commented that the Greeks "gather in their churches extraordinarily often" and that "whoever can spare enough of his possessions for one man to be able to live from their produce makes a church in his own field, vineyard or house, and establishes a priest in it, and his successors [do so] after him." The westerner condemned this easy piety because he saw it as a cover for conspiratorial activities.

All in all, the structure of Byzantine society was such as to make religion something both very intimate and very other-worldly. The truth of this paradox can be appreciated by examining those aspects of the Church's life which were common to both east and west, and yet which gave Byzantine Christianity a distinctive flavor: the liturgy, the monastic life and the pictorial representation of holy persons.

Orthodox liturgy. Anyone who has been to an Orthodox liturgy is in a position to recognize those features which distinguish it from the Roman mass. While both services are in essence celebrations of the Eucharist, with many common formulae, including the reading of the Creed and New Testament texts, the Orthodox service lasts on average one and a half hours, includes many litanies and is punctuated by two major processions and much opening and closing of doors. The hymns are a symbolic commentary upon the plot of a symbolic drama – Christ's passion and resurrection – and are sung without instrumental accompaniment by a choir which at one point claims to represent the Cherubim. The central door in the screen (*templon, iconostasis*) dividing the congregation from the sanctuary represents both the Beautiful Gate of the Temple and the stone at the mouth of Christ's tomb. This cycle of the liturgy itself is only the culmination of a daily cycle including vespers and matins. This routine in turn exists within a cycle of eight weeks, during each of which the hymns are sung in one of eight musical modes. All these cycles merge into the yearly cycle of which the high point is Passion week, where every moment leading to the Resurrection is relived with great color and suspense. Every day of the week the center of the church is held by the icon depicting the event. Judas, the treacherous disciple, is rebuked as if he is present in person. The supreme moment of the Good Friday service celebrates a picturesque paradox: "He who suspended the earth in the waters now hangs upon a piece of wood." The Old Testament is introduced wherever appropriate: Christ's sojourn in hell is elaborately compared with that of Jonah in the belly of the whale.

The Orthodox liturgy of today represents the fusion, completed in the 13th century but prefigured in earlier centuries, of two liturgical traditions: the "cathedral rite" of the town churches, notably St Sophia, and the "monastic rite" which had developed in the monastic communities of the Holy Land and Constantinople. It is the document *par excellence* for a study of the Byzantine mind, being an accretion of all that a conservative people retained from over 1,000 years of existence, as well as from pagan and Jewish antiquity. The liturgical cycle is the work of many famous hands: among others, the Church Fathers St John Chrysostom and St Basil; the hymnographers Romanos the Melodist and St John Damascene. There are hymns attributed to emperors and one, sung to the Virgin during Lent, may commemorate the delivery of Constantinople from the Avar-Slav siege of 626. In a way unparalleled in the west, the Byzantine liturgy became the supreme recreation for all classes of society, a meeting point of folk culture and elite culture comparable to the mystery festivals of pagan Greece. It combined lavish ceremonial worthy of the imperial court (from which it may have been inspired) with simple prayer; it catered to the most mechanical piety while providing a picturesque introduction to some of the most complex theological doctrines.

The monastic movement. The liturgy represented the communion of all believers, the sanctification of all creation before God. The monastic life represented quite the opposite: a flight from worldly society, renunciation of its values and despair at the possibility of salvation except by extraordinary measures. This motive can be seen very clearly in the men who are traditionally regarded as the founders, the desert fathers of 4th-century Egypt. These men, of whom St Anthony was the most famous representative, left one of the most crowded, humdrum existences of the Roman world – the agricultural society of the Nile Delta – for the freedom of the wilderness. The hermit population of the Egyptian desert soon became so large that abuses and eccentricities became cause for concern. This concern led to the foundation of monastic communities, with admission requirements and with a program of worship; this stage is associated above all with St Pachomios. The monastic movement spread northward to Palestine, Syria and Asia Minor. By the early 5th century, monasteries were established in Constantinople.

It was inevitable that, as it became respectable, the monastic life should become less and less a matter of "dropping out" (*anachoresis*) and more and more a matter of social organization. The influential reforms and writings of the 4th-century Church Father St Basil stressed the necessity for communal discipline. Imperial legislation, notably that of Justinian, brought all monks strictly under episcopal control, although this control broke down during iconoclasm and subsequently many houses obtained exemption from it by putting themselves directly under the jurisdiction of the emperor or the patriarch.

The pattern for most middle and late Byzantine monastic houses was the Stoudios monastery in Constantinople. As revitalized in the late 8th century under the direction of its abbot Theodore, this became a highly regulated and businesslike community, where the monks performed specific practical duties. The monastery had one of the largest scriptoria ever to exist in the Byzantine Empire; other monasteries provided equally useful services, such as education and welfare. The typical community (*koinobion*) was built on a rectangular plan around a courtyard, in the center of which was the free-standing monastic church (*katholikon*). Besides the monks' cells, the other buildings comprised a large refectory, a kitchen,

Right: a liturgical roll, beginning with a miniature of St Basil, whose liturgy follows. Patmos 707, 13th century.

Below: symbolic instruments used in the Orthodox Eucharist: illustration from John Covel's *Some Account of the Present Greek Church* (1722). This book was written mainly to correct the opinion, then common in England, that the Greek Church was closer to Protestantism than to Catholicism.

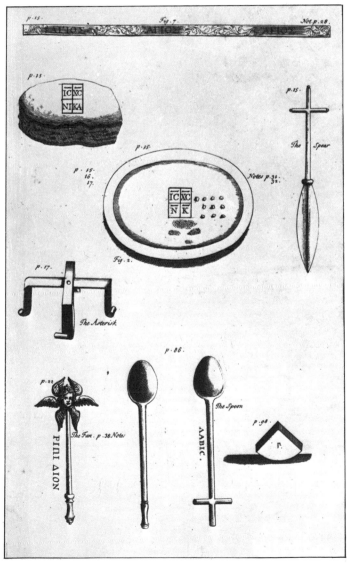

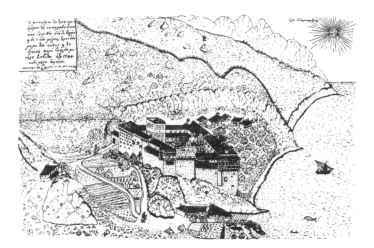

Monasteries on Mount Athos. *Above:* the 14th-century foundation of Dionysiou, from a drawing of 1744. *Opposite:* the monastery of St Panteleimon, founded in the 11th century but whose present buildings date from the early 19th century.

Left: St Simeon the Stylite, from an 11th-century Athos manuscript (Dionysiou 587).

storerooms for agricultural produce, a guest house and an infirmary. If the monastery was in the countryside, it would present a fortified aspect, with high, impenetrable walls and a crenelated gate tower. Altogether, the monastery could resemble a small town. In this, developments in the east ran parallel to those in the west, where the absorbing and varied round of daily work prescribed by St Benedict (6th century) narrowed the gap between monks and laymen. Inevitably, idealists found this type of existence spiritually superficial, yet the solutions in east and west were quite different. The Latin monks reformed by developing some virtuous activity and thus arose the religious orders of the high Middle Ages: the farming Cistercians, the fighting Hospitalers and Templars, the preaching Dominicans and Franciscans. The Byzantines could not believe that spiritual perfection lay in worldly activity. For them, as for the men of late Roman Egypt, *anachoresis* was a flight not from barbarism, ignorance and violence, but from civilization itself. The ideal monk was a recluse who had all the traits of a misanthrope; his ideal dwelling place was the wilderness.

The leading lights in the history of Byzantine monasticism were often good administrators and men of sound practical wisdom but these were not the qualities which made them heroes. The biographies of the founders of some of the major monastic communities describe them as stern and truculent individuals whose preference was for solitary prayer and meditation. They went out of their way to avoid gaining a reputation and discouraged all but the most determined disciples. They lived on the most meager of vegetarian diets, abhorred every female and spoke their minds to the rich and powerful. Their virtues were of the same order as those of the anarchical fringe of Byzantine sainthood: the "fools for Christ" who delighted in public humiliation, and the stylites who lived, year in year out, perched on the tops of columns. The most dedicated monks exploited this sense of being on the fringe by founding their communities in mountain areas, where only shepherds and brigands, the unstable elements in society, normally lived. From the 8th to the 11th century, the spiritual powerhouses of the Orthodox world were the mountains of Olympos and Auxentios in Bithynia, and Latros in Caria. With the Seljuk invasions, these centers declined, except briefly in the Nicaean period. The monastery on the island of Patmos was founded in the 1080s by a refugee from Latros, Christodoulos. The major monastic center in the late Byzantine period was, however, Mount Athos, the "Holy Mountain," whose 20 ruling monasteries are still thoroughly medieval in lifestyle if not in structure. Other European mountain districts became important in the 13th and 14th centuries: Ganos and Paroria in Thrace, Pelion and Meteora in Thessaly.

The role of monasticism. Precisely because it represented a socially acceptable negation of society, Byzantine monasticism fulfilled a vital social role: it affected society at all levels and was in turn affected. The holy man shunned the world, but the world sought him out because he enjoyed familiarity of speech (*parresia*) with God. Thus St Simeon Stylites was consulted as witch doctor and

oracle by the people of Antioch. Andrew, the "Fool for Christ," lived like a crazed derelict in the streets of Constantinople and deliberately hid his sanctity, yet for those who could appreciate him he was a Christian Socrates. When the plague came to Constantinople, the emperor led a procession of supplicants to the column inhabited by Daniel, another well-known stylite. Few could attain such sanctity, but all could try. The monastic vocation was open to all, rich and poor, men and women, young and old. It promised comfort to all who for any reason felt disappointed in life; it also gave many a sense of superiority they could not otherwise have known. Being a monk was its own distinction: no qualifications of wealth, birth or education were necessary, and indeed these things could be impediments to spiritual progress. In turning his back on them, the monk gained a spiritual advantage over the layman and even over his own ecclesiastical superiors, the bishops and patriarch, committed as these were to a measure of worldly activity. The monasteries were therefore the inner bastions of Orthodoxy. The iconoclast controversy was largely a battle between the monks on the one hand and the hierarchies of Church and state on the other; the same division occurred in the 1270s, when Michael VIII tried to commit his people to ecclesiastical union with Rome. The power of the monks became especially apparent in the last two centuries of Byzantium. Bishops were recruited mostly from monasteries. The

appointment of Patriarch Athanasios I solely on the basis of his monastic piety in 1289 was an experiment which aroused strong opposition, but from the middle of the 14th century the Church was firmly in the hands of such patriarchs.

It was in theology, however, that the monks made their strongest impact. In the 14th century a party in the Church led by the monks of Mount Athos succeeded, after bitter controversy, in establishing as Orthodox doctrine the theory that a regime of solitary prayer and fasting known as "quietude" (*hesychia*) could lead men to the vision of the uncreated light observed by Christ's three disciples who were present at His Transfiguration. This mysticism was nothing new: it went back ultimately to Plato and Pythagoras, and in the eastern Christian tradition it had already been publicized by an 11th-century writer, St Symeon the "New Theologian." What was new was the suggestion that it could achieve results which normal sacramental worship and pious living could not. The "Hesychasts," as its practitioners were known, were provoked into defending themselves by a skeptical visitor from southern Italy, Barlaam of Calabria, who insisted that the uncreated light of God could not be seen, and that to claim vision of it was to fall into an old heresy. The Hesychasts found an intellectual spokesman in Gregory Palamas, who answered Barlaam by developing the idea that the light seen by the disciples, and by those mystics who were judged worthy, belonged, although uncreated, to God's "energies" and not to his "essence." All Byzantines regarded Barlaam as an insolent troublemaker, but by no means all of them agreed with Palamas. The outstanding intellectual of the century, Nikephoros Gregoras, and the moderate theologian Gregory Akindynos, fought hard to prevent the Palamite formula from becoming dogma; however, in 1351 the emperor John Kantakouzenos, who was sympathetic to Palamas, convened a synod which condemned his opponents. The vindication of Hesychasm did not affect the Creed or the liturgical worship of the laity; the most popular mystical writer of the late Byzantine period, Nicholas Kabasilas, derived little inspiration from Palamite theology. However, the Hesychast victory meant the triumph of the anti-intellectual tradition within the Church, and reinforced the conviction of all but a few Byzantines that they possessed everything necessary to salvation.

Monks, it was believed, could not achieve the concentration necessary to pray effectively unless they were completely free of all worldly concerns. This made them economically dependent on the generosity of laymen. Laymen did not fail to respond. Whether the Byzantine was hopeful or apprehensive, successful or disappointed, there was no moment in life when he could not benefit from a monk's prayers or might not need a friendly monastery to give him refuge from a world governed by fortune. No bequest was too generous – the early Christians Ananias and Sapheira had, after all, been struck dead by St Peter for having withheld a mere fraction of their property; no reduction in taxes on monastic property was excessive – for "what has once been offered to God cannot be exploited." The monasteries attracted all the benefactions which, in more secular societies, wealthy individuals might have spent in patronage of the arts or in the building of public amenities. This heavy flow of riches from lay to monastic hands was somewhat compensated by the fact that the majority of Byzantine monasteries were short lived, victims of their own chastity, of the greed of raiders and, not infrequently, of their own lay patrons. Nevertheless, by a combination of donation and fiscal concession, the Byzantine lay establishment, and notably the state, alienated in perpetuity resources which were vital for its military defense – not to mention the large number of young men who deprived the state of their services by becoming monks. These facts do not seem to have caused great concern; after iconoclasm, only Alexios I and Manuel II requisitioned monastic property to save an almost desperate military situation. Nikephoros II, who legislated against the foundation of new monasteries, and Manuel I, who founded a monastery with no endowments, aimed to improve the quality of monastic life, not to abolish monastic parasitism. Eustathios, metropolitan of Thessalonica in the late 12th century, wrote a long diatribe against monastic abuses. Yet after condemning the monasteries for overdue preoccupation with money,

agriculture and the pleasures of the table, Eustathios goes on to praise monastic materialism as something potentially beneficial, and cites the example of the emperor Manuel Komnenos who, faced with the necessity of giving a banquet during Lent, and unable to procure sufficient delicacies at short notice, found all that he required in the nearby monastery of St John the Baptist at Petra.

The Byzantines thought of the monastic population as forming a society superior but parallel to their own: a "holy army," a "heavenly city," Looking at the geographical distribution of the monasteries in the Byzantine world, one is led to conclude that they were essentially an urban phenomenon (according to Byzantine urban standards), depending upon prosperous town-dwellers for their existence and reflecting a town's vitality. The major centers – Constantinople, Thessalonica, Nicaea, Trebizond, Athens, Arta, Mistra – had numerous and important monasteries inside and outside their walls. Even where the monasteries lay in apparent isolation, the connection with a local town was no less important. The famous rock monasteries of the Meteora in northwestern Thessaly were founded by men associated with the town of Trikkala, some 14 miles away, at a time when this was a flourishing, independent dynastic capital. Recent research has shown that the monastery of Hosios Loukas, whose present *katholikon* is surprisingly large and splendid for its

isolation in the mountains of central Greece, was closely associated with Thebes, 40 miles away, when this city was at the height of its very considerable prosperity in the 11th and 12th centuries. Even the monasteries of Mount Athos, which attracted patronage and members from all over the Orthodox world and lay almost 100 miles from the nearest city, can be seen from their documents to have shared in the life of Thessalonica and Serres: like these places, Athos was at its most vital in the 14th century. The considerations which influenced the location of a monastery are succinctly expressed by the early 13th-century metropolitan of Naupaktos, John Apokaukos, who wrote of the Blacherna nunnery near Arta that it was near enough to the mountain for the more ambitious nuns to find solitude but close enough to the town for the community to be able to buy clothing and footwear.

The degree to which the Byzantines brought monasticism into the home made a deep and unfavorable impression upon a 14th-century western observer, Brocard.

One of his suggestions for reforming the Byzantine Empire along Latin lines was the following: "that all the monks whom they call Calogeri, that is 'good old men,' should be expelled from the whole empire . . . These Calogeri, wearing simple habits, put on an appearance of great abstinence. By eating certain seeds which draw the color from their cheeks, they make their faces look pallid that they may appear to men to be fasting. By contortions of the neck and face and lowering of the eyes they present a certain image of sanctity, they who are in reality ravenous wolves in sheep's clothing, and like whited sepulchers. So demented do they render the emperor and nobles, the clergy and the entire people, that these believe whatever they say and do whatever they command." Of these "evil customs" which Brocard noted among the Greeks, three concerned the monks: "that it is always a Calogerus who is ordained bishop in every church, and never any secular cleric, however excellent"; "that in the whole empire the only worship is that of these perfidious Calogeri"; "that no secular clergyman, of whatever fame or reputation, hears the confession of any man, but only the Calogeri are appointed to this task."

Icon-worship. In spite of this, the living man of God was too forbidding a figure for everyday comfort. For friendly assurance that all would be well, the Byzantine preferred

Opposite: the Virgin and Child flanked by Sts George and Theodore, with angels behind. The icon, probably of the early 7th century, belongs to the monastery of St Catherine on Mount Sinai. It survived iconoclasm because this region was outside the political jurisdiction of the empire.

Left: the monastic centers of the Byzantine world.

Below: the church of the monastery of the Peribleptos at Mistra (14th century). The interior contains some excellent frescoes.

to turn to beings who had won their earthly battle with the powers of darkness, and might therefore be expected to regard the sins of mankind with a more indulgent eye: Christ and the saints, above all His Mother, the All Holy (*Panagia*) or God-Bearer (*Theotokos*). As we have seen, the presence of the saints was guaranteed by their relics, but these unsightly fragments of human anatomy and clothing could not properly focus the attention of the supplicant. The snapshot evokes the presence of the loved one more surely than the lock of hair; it can also be reproduced *ad infinitum*. Thus it was through the picture or icon (*eikon*) that the Byzantine worshiper came face to face with his saint.

Christianity inherited from Judaism the second Commandment issued to Moses, which forbade the worship of "graven images" and the early Christians had been singled out for persecution because of the insistence with which they refused to pay their respects to the image of the emperor. With the institution of Christianity as the state religion and the personification of the emperor as Christ on earth, such scruples lost their force, and with the final extermination of pagan worship under Justinian, Christians could without embarrassment venerate representations of their own holy beings. Depiction was largely two-dimensional, and it was emphasized that the icon was merely the likeness of a holy being and not itself an object of veneration. Great store was set by authenticity of depiction; characteristically, the most precious Byzantine icon of all, that of the Virgin Hodegetria, was reputed to have been painted by St Luke from the living model. However, it is but a short step from veneration of a spiritual being to veneration of a tangible object, especially in a conservative society which has been deprived of its idolatrous pagan traditions. Thus popular superstition began to endow icons with lives of their own: they could weep, travel, punish and heal. Adulterers turned their bedroom icons to the wall; one Byzantine lady realized she had been bewitched when she prayed to her icons and then found them covered in excrement. Famous icons of the same saint in different places became surrounded by different legends and attributes, just as, in ancient times, Artemis of Ephesus had been almost a different deity from the Artemis of Delos or Brauron.

The potential idolatry of icon-worship was always a matter of concern in early Byzantine society, especially among the Monophysites, who disliked any suggestion that Christ had had a human face. This concern developed into alarm towards the end of the 7th century, when the empire was fighting for its survival against the Arabs, and alarm developed into iconoclasm in the 8th century, when the emperors Leo III and Constantine V made a systematic attempt to abolish religious representations of the human form throughout the empire. In the last chapter we noted the main stages of this policy and its ultimate failure. Here we should briefly consider its significance. It has been reaffirmed convincingly in recent years that the iconoclast controversy must be taken on its face value; that this

The icon of the Virgin Hodegetria carried in procession by the Emperor Michael VIII Palaiologos. This representation on a lead seal alludes to his triumphal entry into Constantinople in 1261.

serious conflict which divided Byzantine society for at least a century and a quarter was not an economic, institutional or racial struggle, but was indeed a dispute about the place of pictures in Christian worship. From what we know of the Byzantine mind, it seems quite likely that a large section of the episcopate and the army, if not of the people as a whole, genuinely believed that the Arab and Slav invasions were God's way of punishing the Romans for their idolatry. The iconoclast emperors may have had other considerations, such as a desire to curb the influence of the monks and a wish to concentrate public opinion on the imperial cult, but they were no doubt equally sincere in their conviction that icons were ungodly.

The iconoclasts eventually lost because they were outnumbered, but they also made less of a case for themselves, arguing as they did that images were consubstantial with their originals. Against this the iconodule apologist John of Damascus objected that the portraits of holy persons who had appeared on earth were symbols which presented their faces but were not identical with their essential personalities. God had made His intentions in the matter quite clear by sending His Son to earth in human form. The whole dispute thus came to center around the issue of the Incarnation, and the iconoclasts were driven to adopt a position akin to that of the Monophysites.

Both eastern and western Christendom were represented in the council of 787 which rehabilitated the cult of images, yet the conflict was essentially internal to Byzantium. In the west there had been no passionate attachment to icons and no violent reaction against them. Charlemagne – who felt no commitment to a council held by his imperial rivals – was content to declare that images were not essential to salvation. This was important for the development of religious art in the west, because being denied intercessory power, it was subject to less retraint.

Iconography of the icon. We tend to think of the icon as a painted wooden panel of portable dimensions kept in the home or paraded in procession, and indeed the most precious Orthodox icons are of this kind. Yet the mosaic and fresco decorations which covered the walls of every Byzantine church were also cycles of icons. In early

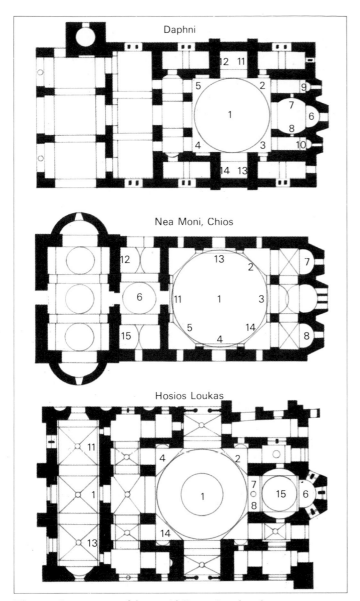

The mosaic programs of three mid-Byzantine churches.
1 Pantokrator, 2 Annunciation, 3 Birth of Christ, 4 Baptism of Christ,
5 Transfiguration, 6 Madonna with Child, 7 Michael, 8 Gabriel, 9 John
the Baptist, 10 Nikolaos, 11 Crucifixion, 12 Entry into Jerusalem,
13 Resurrection, 14 Presentation, 15 Descent of the Holy Spirit. After
Diez-Demus.

four pendentives was the figure of an evangelist. The vaults
forming the arms of the cross contained the 12 major feasts
in the life of Christ (*Dodekaeorton*); pride of place was given
to the Ascension, over the sanctuary, with the figure of
Christ occupying the crown of the hemicylindrical vault
and the Apostles ranged six on either side. The conch of
the apse at the east end of the building, the main focus of
the interior after the dome, showed the Virgin enthroned
with the infant Jesus seated on her lap. The lower levels of
the building were free to be decorated with other scenes
from the life of Christ and portraits of individual saints.

The iconographical cycle was unchanging only to the
extent that a certain symmetry and gradation had to be
observed according to Orthodox dogma. But there was
infinite room for variation. The taste for scenes as opposed
to portraits was one which developed with time. Only
relatively modest churches were painted from top to
bottom; the lower wall-surfaces in a *de luxe* church, such
as Hosios Loukas, were covered with marble revetment
like Justinian's Hagia Sophia. If the architecture was
intended to highlight the wall-painting, it also happened
that a new architectural form called for adjustments in the
icon program. The accompanying plans of the three
"classic" Byzantine monuments – Hosios Loukas, Nea
Moni and Daphni – illustrate this most clearly: for
example, the lack of transepts at Nea Moni has brought
eight of the scenes from Christ's life under the dome, with
the other four relegated to the narthex; the presence of
squinches rather than pendentives under the domes at
Daphni and Hosios Loukas demands the representation
of scenes here in preference to single portraits. The rein-
troduction of the basilican plan in the later Byzantine
period called for rearrangements on the upper level, as
well as for subjects appropriate to flat surfaces. Finally, the
founder's taste and the purpose of the building were
factors which could determine the prominence, the
inclusion and the location of certain subjects.

Byzantine artists and patrons have left few written
records of themselves which give explicit information
about the traditions, techniques and sociology of Byzantine religious art. The incidence of mosaic and fresco
suggests that the former was preferred as a medium but
was more expensive. For the sake of convenience, most
representation can be seen as belonging to one of two
traditions: a "Hellenistic" mode, which combined variety
and subtlety of color with naturalistic treatment of perspective, drapery and the human form; and an "abstract"
mode, which tended not to blend colors, and showed
human figures as frontal, incorporeal and expressionless.
The general pattern of evolution is clear: the portrayal of
self-contained, monumental figures against plain gold or
blue backgrounds gave way to a fashion for animated
scenes where no character seems larger than life and there
is a wealth of background architecture and picturesque
costume. But dates and artists are hard to identify on
purely stylistic grounds. The working relationship of

Byzantine church decoration, there is much material that
is strictly non-iconic: symbolic vegetation, the plain
symbol of the cross, prominent portraits of emperors and
bishops. Justinian's church of Hagia Sophia may not have
contained any figural decoration. With the defeat of
iconoclasm, however, a rigorous program was instituted.
The Church now became a model of the heavenly
hierarchy. The standard form of architecture, the cross-in-
square crowned by a dome (see Visual Story 4), lent itself
particularly well to this scheme. The spherical surface in
the dome was occupied by the bust of Christ, gazing down
upon His people as a somber teacher and judge. As if to
support this image of the Almighty, prophets and/or
angels stood around the drum of the dome. On each of the

mosaicists to wall-painters; the pioneer role of manuscript illuminators; the differences between "metropolitan" and "provincial" art; the existence of "schools": these are all factors about which general assumptions are premature. Some of the best-known monuments of Byzantine art are also the most elusive. The mosaics of Hosios Loukas have usually been assigned to the 11th century, but a recent analysis based mainly upon hagiographical texts has argued for a late 10th-century date. The *Deesis* panel of Hagia Sophia is now generally reckoned to be a work of Michael VIII's reign, but a late 12th-century date is still entertained.

Byzantine religious painting deserves to be regarded as the most successful Christian artform ever created. One is naturally curious as to how the Byzantines perceived their visual productions. From this point of view, Byzantine authors can be disappointing if searched for "art criticism." Byzantine *ekphraseis* or literary celebrations of works of art can be useful as evidence for monuments no longer existing, or for the context in which some were put up; they also confirm that most discussion of Byzantine aesthetics is conducted in terms which the Byzantines themselves did not express. There was no market in

Below: military and hunting scenes, no doubt similar in style to those depicted in the mosaic cycles of Byzantine secular palaces, from an ivory casket at Troyes.

Above: a pair of 7th-century Byzantine earrings.

Opposite: the lion hunt. A Byzantine tapestry of the 13th century. Vatican Library.

Byzantium for adverse criticism, and panegyrists were less concerned to praise what they saw on its visual merits than to identify with an ancient literary tradition according to which art was good if it was true to nature.

Minor and secular arts. Sculpture was not a standard medium of religious iconography; in churches it was reserved for those parts of the building which were usually of stone – column capitals, door jambs, the screen, the ambo, the ciborium – and it generally used non-human designs, such as mythical beasts, geometric designs and plant motifs. But the full range of Christian subject-matter was treated by other craftsmen – gold and silver smiths, enamel workers, ivory carvers, jewelers, embroiderers, manuscript illuminators – who produced all the objects used in the liturgy, as well as those which the rich commissioned for their private devotions.

The Byzantine monumental art which we see is so overwhelmingly religious in nature that it is easy to forget that there existed in Constantinople a flourishing secular artistic tradition. The written sources show that when imperial or noble palaces were built or renovated it was not uncommon for the walls to be decorated with narrative scenes from popular romances or from the exploits of the reigning emperor. The idealized Byzantine warrior, Digenes Akritas, included Old Testament, Classical and Christian scenes in the decoration of his fabled palace on the Euphrates. Constantine VII, in his *Life of Basil I*, describes the mosaics with which his hero ornamented his addition to the great palace: "From the columns up to [the top of] the ceiling as well as in its eastern dome the entire building has been beautified with gold mosaic cubes; it exhibits the originator of this work seated aloft, escorted by the subordinate generals who fought on his side, the latter offering him in gift the towns they have captured. In addition, high up in the ceiling are depicted the emperor's Herculean labors, his toils on behalf of his subjects, his warlike exertions and the prize of victory bestowed by God." Niketas Choniates, the historian of the period 1118–1204, includes the following details of his account of Andronikos I: "Finally, he erected magnificent quarters for his own use at the shrine of the Forty Martyrs, wherein he was to dwell whenever he visited the shrine. Not having any recent actions suitable to be depicted in these buildings either in blended paints or fine mosaic cubes, he had recourse to his deeds prior to his becoming emperor; and so were represented here horse-races and hunts, birds clucking, dogs barking, the capture of deer and hares, wild boar with projecting tusks being transfixed, and the *zubros* being pierced with a spear (this is a beast larger than the mythical bear and the spotted leopard and is reared especially among the Tauroscythians), a rustic life under tents, the informal consumption of the hunted game, Andronikos himself cutting up with his own hand the flesh of deer or solitary boar and cooking it skilfully on the fire . . ."

The Development of the Byzantine Church

Thessalonica was founded in the 4th century BC by Cassander, king of Macedonia. Its position on a sheltered gulf at a point where one of the major access routes to the Mediterranean Sea from the Danubian basin crossed the Via Egnatia, the major east-west highway from the Adriatic to Asia Minor, soon made it the greatest city in the Balkans. The transfer of the seat of imperial government from Rome to Byzantium did not affect its prosperity, and in the middle and late Byzantine periods it was the only provincial center in the empire known as a "great city" (*megalopolis*). The Christian tradition of Thessalonica dates from the missionary visit of Paul the Apostle. Despite the many natural disasters which have affected the urban landscape, and the long Turkish occupation, which transformed the larger churches into mosques, the city retains as representative a selection of Byzantine ecclesiastical monuments as can be seen in any one place.

1. The Rotunda (St George)

Below, in a 19th-century engraving by Texier; *opposite below*, the exterior as seen today. Excavation has revealed that this building was originally attached to the imperial palace which the Tetrarch Galerius built c. 300 AD. Christian roof mosaics (*opposite above*) show that it had been converted into a church by the mid-5th century. Both its secular and its ecclesiastical functions are unclear, since there is no explicit reference to it in any Byzantine source. It was converted into a mosque around the end of the 16th century, became a church again in 1912, and is now a museum.

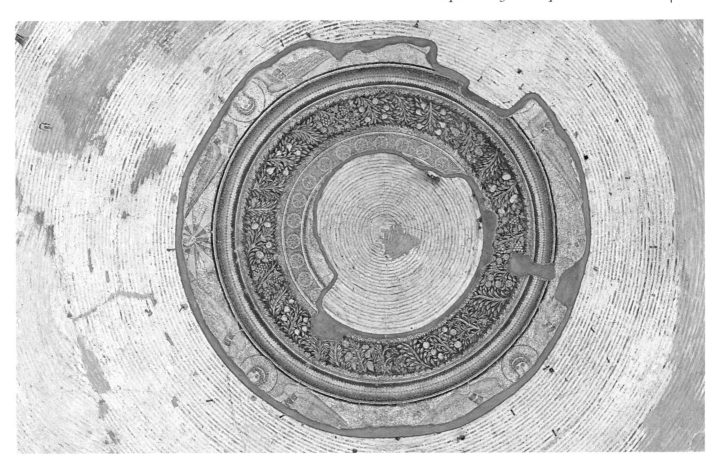

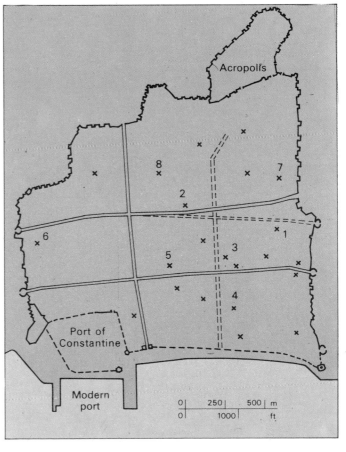

Right: plan of the Byzantine town. After
Theocharides. 1 Rotunda (St George),
2 Basilica of St Demetrios, 3 Basilica of
the Theotokos "Acheiropoietos",
4 Hagia Sophia, 5 Panagia tōn Chalkeōn,
6 Church of the Holy Apostles, 7 St
Nikolaos Orphanos, 8 Church of the
Prophet Elias.

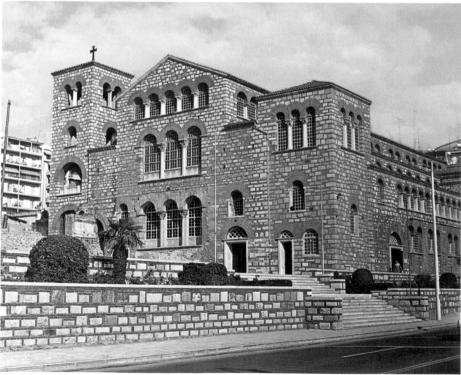

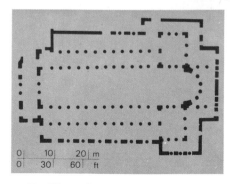

2. Basilica of St Demetrios
Demetrios was a Christian, martyred, probably at Sirmium on the Danube, about 300 AD. After Sirmium was destroyed by the Huns in 441, his cult moved to Thessalonica, and became

centered on the basilica which was built in the 440s by a prefect named Leontius. Although largely destroyed by fire about 630, it was soon rebuilt and as such survived until the great fire of 1917 in which much of the town perished. Prior to the modern reconstruction (*far left*), the building was subjected to extensive archaeological investigation. The plan of the original church (*left*, after Mango), a five-aisled basilica with transept and gallery, can still be discerned and some (later) frescoes are preserved (e.g. St Joasaph on the first pillar on the right, *opposite above*).

3. Basilica of the Theotokos "Acheiropoietos" (Hagia Paraskeve)

A three-aisled basilica also dating from the 440s. On the plan (*right*, after Mango) note (1) the lack of any central door in the west wall of the narthex; (2) the raised stylobate supporting the columns. The church was one of the most important in the liturgical life of Thessalonica, but repeated restoration has stripped most of the original fabric. There are, however, some 5th-century mosaics still visible under the arcades of the gallery and the ground floor (*above*). The monolithic columns are surmounted by Corinthian capitals on the ground level and by Ionic capitals with imposts on the upper level. The church was partly built on the site of

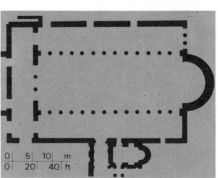

a Roman villa and a fragment of its mosaic flooring is preserved at the end of the left hand nave.

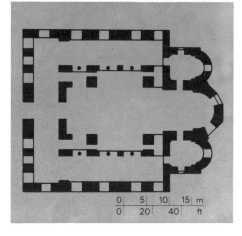

4. Hagia Sophia

This church, which served as the metropolitan church of Thessalonica in the Middle Ages, dates from no later, and probably from not much earlier, than the reign of Constantine VI and Irene (780–97) who are commemorated in an inscription in the sanctuary. With its *prothesis* and *diakonikon* flanking the sanctuary (*bema*) (see the plan *above*, after Mango), and with its four pilasters (*left*) carrying the dome within the area of the

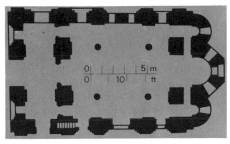

nave, it represents a development from the domed basilica of Hagia Sophia in Constantinople, yet its north and south galleries and the absence of transverse vaults mark its similarity to the Justinianic structure. It was built over the site of a 5th-century basilica of colossal proportions (more than 100 meters long), which formed part of the mid-5th-century refurbishing of the city.

5. Panagia tōn Chalkeōn

The classic church structure of the middle Byzantine period, the "inscribed Greek cross" or "domed cross in square," is represented in Thessalonica by this church built in 1028 (plan *above*, after Mango). The square is formed by the nave of the church, i.e. the area between the sanctuary and the narthex. The arms of the cross are formed at roof level by the vaults adjoining the dome, and its inner corners by the four columns on which the dome rests. Note the polygonal (as opposed to cylindrical) drum underneath the dome: this feature, which originated probably in 7th-century Armenia and appeared in Byzantium at the end of the 10th century, allowed greater amplification of both drum and dome. The excellent frescoes in the narthex and sanctuary (*right*) are contemporary with the church.

6. Church of the Holy Apostles

This church (illustrated *above*) was built in 1310–14 by the patriarch of Constantinople, Niphon. Recent analysis (see the plan, *opposite above*, after Krautheimer) has shown that the masonry points to two phases of construction: (1) the conventional cross-in-square church with dome and narthex; (2) the four-domed exonarthex and ambulatory which envelops the core on three sides. Note the decorative brickwork and the elevation of the central structure relative to its area. As an ensemble, the building continues trends exhibited in earlier Palaiologan churches, including its own neighbor in Thessalonica, Hagia Aikaterine, and foreshadows the more harmonious and ambitious Serbian monastery church of Gračanica.

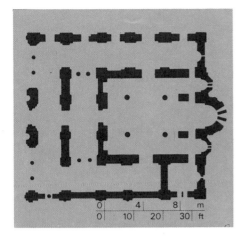

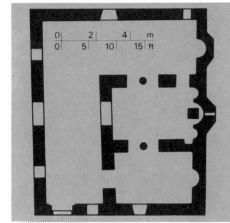

7. St Nikolaos Orphanos

An early 14th-century foundation, this
small monastery church (illustrated
opposite below) is more remarkable for its
paintings (*right*) than for its architecture. It
may, however, serve here as an example
of the many non-domed, basilican
churches which were built in the Balkans
from the 11th century onwards. The
unusually large ambulatory-cum-
exonarthex (see the plan, *above*, after
Xyngopoulos) no doubt served the same
purpose as in other Palaiologan churches.

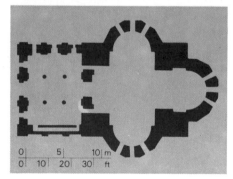

8. Church of the Prophet Elias

This church is remarkable for its elaborate brickwork and for the semicircular shape of its transepts (see the plan, after Mango) – a feature which is normally associated with the churches of Mt Athos, and demonstrates the great influence of that monastic center on the society of Thessalonica in the 14th century. The church may have belonged to the monastery of Nea Moni, founded between 1360 and 1370 by the monk Makarios Choumnos.

6. The Byzantine Achievement

URBS CONSTANTINOPOLITANA NOVA ROMA.

What did Byzantium achieve? What is it worth to us? General assessments of Byzantine society tend implicitly to answer these two questions as if they were one, and to make the verdict depend on the author's own attitude to the second question. However, it is possible to entertain a variety of personal opinions about Byzantium and still to arrive at a fairly standard evaluation of its material achievements. Statistically the results are impressive. The Eastern Roman Empire maintained a continuous existence for over 1,000 years, during which it suffered no radical constitutional change and kept the same capital, except for the half-century of the Latin Empire. At its apogee it ruled the whole of Asia Minor and the Balkan peninsula. During late antiquity and the Dark Ages it sustained barbarian inroads as devastating as any which affected western Europe, and at all times it bore the brunt of the fighting with the powerful empires of the Middle East. From the 9th century and throughout the long slow decline of its last 400 years, the civilization of Constantinople was the dominant cultural influence in the Balkans, Russia and occasionally in other parts of eastern Europe. It adopted more primitive social structures and settlement patterns without losing its legal, economic and literary traditions. Hardly any of its rulers lacked a flair for either administration, or war or diplomacy, and a surprising number of them combined ability in all three. All in all, few states have ever shown so long or so distinguished a record.

The judgment of history would probably have been content to leave it at that were Byzantium a culture as alien to our own as imperial China or pharaonic Egypt. As it happens, the Roman, Greek and Christian elements in Byzantine civilization are also major strands in western European culture. Byzantine studies in the west have thus started from the double premise that Byzantium was good insofar as it transmitted these elements to modern Europe, and bad insofar as it made different use of them.

The Roman element. The "Roman inheritance" was a burning question in the Middle Ages, when men could not conceive of a higher form of political authority than the Roman emperor. The basic continuity of the Eastern Empire is a fact which no modern scholar would dispute, and which caused endless embarrassment to the papacy and to the Germanic monarchs who took the imperial title. Westerners solved the dilemma by calling the ruler in Constantinople "emperor of the Greeks." This pejorative expression attributed to the Byzantine Empire an ethnicity which it did not quite possess; still, it accurately reflected the fact that the medieval state functioned as a cultural unit, and not as a polyglot federation of cities and tribes such as the Classical Roman Empire had been. Byzantium undoubtedly inspired the image which the western emperors, especially Otto, fashioned for them-

Previous page: the city of Constantinople from a 15th-century manuscript of the *Notitia Dignitatum*. Bodleian Library, Oxford.

selves, and the coronation ceremonies of other western monarchies may have derived from Constantinople. In general, however, the most beneficial elements in the Roman tradition – Roman law and Latin literature – were transmitted to modern Europe by the western Church. The direct political heirs of Byzantium in the modern world were the Russian and Ottoman empires.

The Greek element. Since the 17th century, the Greek heritage in Byzantium has received rather more scholarly attention because, as was mentioned earlier, knowledge of the Greek classics was transmitted through Constantinople. For an enlightened intellectual milieu which believed that its own outstanding achievements were somehow connected with the fairly recent revival of Classical studies, it seemed incredible that the Byzantines could have read the same literature for 1,000 years and yet failed to make any advance on the ancient world. The sense of shock is expressed most forcefully by Edward Gibbon, the late 18th-century historian of the *Decline and Fall of the Roman Empire*:

"Not a single idea has been added to the speculative systems of antiquity, and a succession of patient disciples became in their turn the dogmatic teachers of the next servile generation. Not a single composition of history, philosophy, or literature, has been saved from oblivion by the intrinsic beauties of style or sentiment, of original fancy, or even of successful imitation. In prose, the least offensive of the Byzantine writers are absolved from censure by their naked and unpresuming simplicity; but the orators, most eloquent in their own conceit, are the farthest removed from the models whom they affect to emulate. In every page our taste and reason are wounded by the choice of gigantic and obsolete words, a stiff and intricate phraseology, the discord of images, the childish play of false or unseasonable ornament, and the painful attempt to elevate themselves, to astonish the reader, and to involve a trivial meaning in the smoke of obscurity and exaggeration . . . The minds of the Greeks were bound in the fetters of a base and imperious superstition, which extends her dominion round the circle of profane science. Their understandings were bewildered in metaphysical controversy; in the belief of visions and miracles, they had lost all principles of moral evidence; and their taste was vitiated by the homilies of the monks, an absurd medley of declamation and scripture. Even these contemptible studies were no longer dignified by the abuse of superior talents; the leaders of the Greek church were humbly content to admire and copy the oracles of antiquity, nor did the schools or pulpit produce any rivals of the fame of Athanasius and Chrysostom."

This interpretation may not be entirely acceptable, but it may be doubted whether 200 years of research have done much to make Byzantine literature more enjoyable or intellectually stimulating. And the explanation is plausible: the monolithic structure of Byzantium stifled

St Sophia, Constantinople, built by Justinian in the 6th century, perhaps the most glorious monument to Byzantine civilization.

individual creativity, whereas the disunity of the west promoted this.

Gibbon's anti-Christian attitude was controversial in his native England, but his aversion to Byzantine piety has been shared by many western Christians, both Protestant and Catholic. We have already noted the western attitude to Byzantine monasticism: Brocard's comments could have been written by a French or English antiquary of the 19th century. Fundamental to this antipathy was a moral contempt for the behavior of the Greeks – a contempt which had long ago found expression in the Roman poet Juvenal's vilification of the "wheedling Greek." The experience of the Crusades confirmed the worst of western prejudices. Not only did the Byzantines obstruct the crusading movement but they did so with a suavity which to the simple, impulsive westerners seemed to be the purest kind of knavery, although it had long been Byzantine diplomatic practice.

Odo of Deuil, who chronicled the French king Louis VII's part in the Second Crusade, tells how when the crusading army approached Constantinople the Greeks were at first hostile, but when the empress established contact with the French queen, "then the Greeks were

inwardly reduced to women, putting aside all manly fiber of word and spirit. They lightly promised whatever they thought we wanted, but they kept neither good faith nor integrity. The opinion is widespread among them that no perjury is to be held to account which is committed for the sake of their holy empire. And let none think that I am hatefully attacking one race of men, and by hatred of them inventing things which I have not seen, for if you question anyone who has known the Greeks, he will agree that when they are afraid they grovel in utter dejection, and when they have the upper hand are overbearing in the heavy oppression of those subject to them." When the crusaders reached Constantinople their suspicions were further aroused by the blandishments offered them. One bishop proposed taking the city by force "because it does not have the substance of Christianity but only the name." Although the idea was taken seriously, it took another half-century of deepening mutual mistrust before it was realized.

The plight of the Byzantines in the years of their final decline did not move westerners to any greater sympathy. The Spaniard Pero Tafur, recalling his visit to Constantinople in the 1430s, wrote: "The inhabitants are not well clad, but sad and poor, showing the hardship of their lot which is, however, not so bad as they deserve, for they are a vicious people, steeped in sin."

The further the European intellectual climate became removed from that of the Middle Ages, the more sinister Byzantium appeared. Greater distance has lent greater enchantment to the view. According to the editor of the English translation of Charles Diehl's book *Byzance, grandeur et misère* (Paris, 1919), "we have gone far since the eighteenth century, when it was thought that 'the history of the Byzantine empire is nothing but a tissue of revolts, seditions, and perfidies' (Montesquieu), 'a tedious and uniform tale of weakness and misery' (Gibbon), or 'a monotonous story of the intrigues of priests, eunuchs, and women, of poisonings, of conspiracies, of uniform ingratitude, of perpetual fratricide' (Lecky)." But even Diehl – who was regarded as enough of a Byzantine apologist for his name to be given to a street in Thessalonica – felt obliged to make the following moral pronouncement on the Byzantines: "Yet certain traits recur in the best of them: impulsiveness, enthusiasm, a high-strung, impressionable temperament, inordinate ambition, and a love of subtlety and intrigue; all of which resulted in

Above: St Mark's Cathedral in Venice owes much to Byzantine styles of architecture. *Opposite:* one of several capitals removed from the church of St Polyeuktos at Constantinople after the Fourth Crusade and built into the west end of St Mark's.

conduct that too often smacked of unscrupulousness and double-dealing, and above all a weakness of character in contrast to strength of intellect. We feel that the race bore the burden of too weighty a past, that their energies were quickly dissipated, and that their character lacked moral foundations." Happily for the modern Byzantinist, moral judgments are no longer fashionable or easy.

The Christian element. The absolute sincerity of the Byzantines' devotion to the Christian faith, however, is something which need no longer be questioned. Indeed the way in which they continued to endow monasteries, engage in doctrinal disputes, and refuse union with the western Church down to the very fall of their capital suggests that they quite willingly paid the price of political extinction in order to preserve the integrity of their relationship with God. Perhaps the most valuable contri-

bution which Byzantium has to make to modern civilization is the example of a Church which chose the apparently less exemplary part of Mary because it had faith that eternity could be approached here and now. Not that the Church suffered material loss from the fall of the Christian empire. The Ottoman sultans, influenced by both Islamic law and their own considerations of policy, permitted their Christian subjects freedom of worship, and granted monasteries and bishoprics fairly secure tenure of landed property. The patriarch of Constantinople was recognized as leader of all the Christian communities in the Ottoman Empire, whatever their languages, and his was the highest jurisdiction next to the sultan's in all cases involving Christians.

Around the patriarchate there grew up, in the 16th and 17th centuries, a coterie of Greek families, known as the Phanariots from the quarter of Phanari (Fener) in which the patriarchate eventually settled. The Phanariots made huge fortunes in trade and became influential at the Saray by acting as interpreters (dragomans) between the sultans and European ambassadors. They became valuable to the Ottomans both in this capacity and as agents in the empire's Romanian satellites, the principalities of Moldavia and Wallachia. From the late 17th century they dominated the princely courts of Iaşi and Bucharest. Here and in Constantinople they perpetuated the Byzantine cultural tradition, even claiming descent from Byzantine aristocratic families. Their involvement with the Ottoman establishment was too great for them to be altogether wholehearted in their support of nationalist aspirations; the ideological impetus for Greek independence came from western Europe. However, at a popular level it was the Church which provided the forces for nationalist leaders to harness. One of the early poems of Constantine Cavafy, "In Church," expresses the emotive force of Byzantium, and Orthodoxy, for the modern Greek:

> I love the church – its *hexapteryga* [processional disks
>   engraved with the six-winged symbols of the
>   Cherubim],
> the silver of its vessels, its candlesticks,
> its lamps, its icons, and its ambo.
>
> As I enter there, in the church of the Greeks,
> with the sweet fragrance of its incenses,
> with its liturgical chanting and recitals,
> the majestic figures of the priests
> with the solemn rhythm of their every movement,
> resplendent in the decorum of their vestments
> – my mind goes to the great honors of our race,
> to our most glorious Byzantine heritage.

The legacy of Byzantium. Through their language, and through the continuity of the patriarchate, the Greeks have as good a claim as any nation to the problematic heritage of Byzantium. But they are not alone. The medieval history of modern Bulgaria is the history of the first and second Bulgarian empires, the first deliberate imitations of the Byzantine monarchy. Modern Yugoslavia unites many traditions, but the most heroic of these is that of Orthodox Serbia, which traces its existence back to Stephen Dušan, the 14th-century "Emperor of the Serbs and Greeks," and to his 12th-century ancestor, Stephen Nemanja the "first-crowned," founder of one of the most flourishing monasteries on Mount Athos, Chilandar. The epic years of the Romanian principalities belong to the Byzantine aftermath, and the latter-day Byzantium of the Phanariot courts was an alien regime in which few Romanians shared; even so, the national tradition of Romania has been Orthodox. The legend of Cyril and Methodius, the "apostles of the Slavs," has added a Byzantine chapter to the history of Czechoslovakia, and the diplomatic contacts between the Komnenos dynasty and the early kings of Hungary have left their

Above: Christ Pantokrator. A 12th-century mosaic in the apse of the cathedral at Cefalù, Sicily.

The painted churches of Romania. *Right:* Voroneţ (1488–1547), commemorating Stephen the Great's victory over the Turks.
Opposite: Moldviţa (1532–37), depicting the siege of Constantinople.

mark on the Hungarian memory. Byzantium played a major part in the conversion and civilization of Russia. Before and after the period of Mongol domination in the 13th and 14th centuries, Byzantine priests and artists were active in Kiev and Novgorod. After 1461 it was the grand princes of Muscovy and their successors as tsars of Russia who claimed to rule the true Orthodox empire. Besides the Russians and the Ukrainians, the USSR contains two minority groups, the Georgians and the Armenians (the latter being also widely dispersed throughout the world), whose medieval kingdoms were intimately connected with Byzantium. Finally, in the west, one should not neglect to mention the island of Sicily, whose highly cross-fertilized culture contains one Byzantine strain.

For all these countries, Byzantium is one, often the only, common element in their past, and historical research brings their scholars to medieval Constantinople as naturally as it brings western Europeans to the civilization of medieval Rome, Paris or Florence. Historical perspectives in eastern Europe have often been warped by nationalistic passions, but correctives have never been wanting, whether from rival nationalists or from scholars in the western tradition whose prejudices lie elsewhere.

Byzantium played a major part in the conversion and civilization of Russia. *Right*: an icon from the Russian Museum, Leningrad. *Below*: the Cathedral of the Nativity, Suzdal.

Further Reading

Amand de Mendieta, E., *Mount Athos* (Berlin/Amsterdam, 1972).

Baynes, N. H. and **Moss, H. St. L. B.,** *Byzantium. An Introduction to East Roman Civilisation* (Oxford, 1948).

Bovini, G., *Ravenna* (Cologne, 1971).

Brown, P., *The World of Late Antiquity* (London, 1971).

Browning, R., *Medieval and Modern Greek* (London, 1969).

Bury, J. B., *History of the Later Roman Empire*, 2 vols. (London, 1923).

Byzantine Books and Bookmen (Dumbarton Oaks Colloquium; Washington, D.C., 1975).

Cambridge Mediaeval History, 8 vols. (Cambridge, 1911–67).

Constantelos, D. J., *Byzantine Philanthropy and Social Welfare* (New Brunswick, N.J., 1968).

Demus, O., *Byzantine Mosaic Decoration* (London, 1948).

Diehl, C., *L'Afrique byzantine* (Paris, 1896).

—— *Justinien et la civilisation byzantine au VIe siècle* (Paris, 1901).

—— *Byzantine Portraits* (New York, 1927).

—— *Byzantium, Greatness and Decline* (New Brunswick, N.J., 1957).

Downey, G., *A History of Antioch in Syria* (Princeton, N.J., 1961).

Foss, C., "The Persians in Asia Minor and the End of Antiquity," *English Historical Review*, 1975.

—— *Byzantine and Turkish Sardis* (Cambridge, Mass., 1976).

Frend, W., *The Donatist Church* (Oxford, 1952).

Gibbon, E., *The Decline and Fall of the Roman Empire* (Everyman edn., London, 1960).

Grierson, P., *Catalogue of the Byzantine Coins in the Dumbarton Oaks Collection and in the Whittemore Collection*, II.1 (Washington, D.C., 1968), 3–143.

Jenkins, R., *Byzantium, The Imperial Centuries* (London, 1966).

Jones, A. H. M., *Constantine and the Conversion of Europe* (London, 1970).

—— *The Decline of the Ancient World* (London, 1966).

—— *The Later Roman Empire*, 3 vols. (Oxford, 1964).

Krautheimer, R., *Early Christian and Byzantine Architecture* (Harmondsworth, 1975).

Lemerle, P., *Le Premier Humanisme byzantin* (Paris, 1972).

Lot, F., *The End of the Ancient World and the Beginnings of the Middle Ages* (London, 1931).

MacKendrick, P., *The Iberian Stones Speak* (New York, 1969).

—— *Roman France* (London, 1972).

—— *The Dacian Stones Speak* (Chapel Hill, N.C., 1975).

Mango, C., *The Art of the Byzantine Empire, 312–1453 (Sources and Documents)* (Englewood Cliffs, N.J., 1972).

—— *Byzantine Architecture* (London, 1976).

Meyendorff, J., *Byzantine Theology* (New York, 1974).

Obolensky, D., *The Byzantine Commonwealth, Eastern Europe, 500–1453* (London/New York, 1971).

Ostrogorsky, G., *History of the Byzantine State*, tr. J. Hussey (Oxford, 1968).

Piganiol, A., *L'Empire chrétien* (Paris, 1972).

Raven, S., *Rome in Africa* (London, 1969).

Richmond, I. A., *Roman Britain* (London, 1963).

Runciman, S., *Byzantine Civilisation* (London, 1933).

Stein, E., *Histoire du Bas-Empire*, 2 vols. (Paris, 1949, 1959).

Tchalenko, G., *Villages antiques de la Syrie du nord* (Paris, 1953).

Underwood, P. A., ed., *The Kariye Djami*, IV (Princeton, N.J., 1975).

Whitting, P., ed., *Byzantium. An Introduction* (Oxford, 1971).

Acknowledgments

Unless otherwise stated all the illustrations on a given page are credited to the same source.

Archaeological Museum, Istanbul 63 (left)
Ashmolean Museum, Oxford, frontispiece, 20 (top), 35 (bottom), 120
Dick Barnard, London 50 (top), 52
Bibliothèque Nationale, Paris 90; Cabinet des Medailles 28
Bodleian Library, Oxford 35 (top), 111 (left), 129
British Crown Copyright, reproduced with permission of the Controller of HMSO 50 (bottom)
British Library, Department of Manuscripts 48 (top), 80, 92
British Museum, Department of Prints and Drawings 57 (bottom)
Errol Bryant, London 41, 42 (top)
Dumbarton Oaks (Trustees for Harvard University), Washington 83, 89 (bottom), 91 (bottom), 112 (right)
Ekdotike Athenon, S. A., Athens 11, 14, 70, 104, 107 (left and bottom right), 112 (left), 113
Elsevier Archives, Amsterdam 39 (bottom), 64, 97, 114
Mary Evans Picture Library, London 15, 17
Clive Foss, Boston 22, 27, 40, 48 (bottom), 54, 65 (bottom), 67 (top), 78 (bottom), 86 (bottom), 89 (top), 99 (top and center)
Ray Gardner, London 23 (right), 24, 32, 65 (top)
Richard Goodchild; *Illustrated London News* 55
Roger Gorringe, London 39 (top), 44 (top), 47 (top), 61, 73 (top), 101 (top), 117
Sonia Halliday Photographs, Weston Turville 9, 12, 26 (right), 31, 34, 36, 37, 44 (bottom), 45, 47 (bottom), 49, 60 (top), 63 (right), 73 (bottom), 74 (top and center), 75 (top left and bottom), 76 (top and bottom right), 77, 78 (top), 85, 86 (top), 87, 95, 96 (bottom), 100, 101 (bottom), 105, 106, 107 (top right), 115 (bottom), 131; photo by P. Grice 69; colored by Laura Lushington 18, 62; photo by F. H. C. Birch 43, 57 (top), 98 (bottom)
Hannibal, Athens 85
Robert Harding Associates, London 68, 71 (bottom), 133, 135 (bottom), 136

A. A. M. van der Heyden, Amsterdam 56, 57 (top), 91 (top), 122 (bottom left)
Hirmer Verlag, Munich 94 (left), 109, 111 (right), 119 (top)
Historical Picture Service, Brentwood 51
Michael Holford Library, Loughton 119 (bottom)
Israel Department of Antiquities, Jerusalem 71 (top)
Nikos Kontos, Athens 20 (bottom), 60 (bottom), 121 (top and bottom left), 122 (top left), 123 (top), 124 (top and bottom left), 125 (top right and bottom), 126 (bottom), 127 (right), 128 (top)
Lovell Johns, Oxford 10, 99 (bottom), 115 (top)
Mansell Collection, London 13, 25, 29
Bildarchiv Foto Marburg, Marburg 53
National Library, Madrid 102, 103
National Library, Vienna 93, 108
Oxford Illustrators Ltd, Oxford 67 (bottom), 74 (bottom), 75 (top right), 76 (bottom left), 121 (bottom right), 122 (bottom right), 123 (bottom), 124 (bottom right), 125 (top left), 127 (left), 128 (bottom)
Phaidon Press Archive, Oxford 46 (bottom)
Scala, Florence 23 (left), 26 (left), 58, 79, 118, 126 (top), 134 (bottom), 135 (top)
R. V. Schoder, S. J., Chicago 42 (bottom)
Ihor Ševčenko, Cambridge, Mass. 94 (right)
Kenneth Smith, London 98 (top)
G. Speake, Oxford 46 (top), 96 (top)
M. Vickers, Oxford 132 (left)
Walker Trust; by courtesy of the Chairman, D. F. O. Russell 21 (bottom), 33
D. Winfield, Oxford; by courtesy of Dumbarton Oaks (Trustees for Harvard University), Washington 19 (right)
G. Zacos, Basel 116

The Publishers have attempted to observe the legal requirements with respect to the rights of the suppliers of photographic materials. Nevertheless, persons who have claims are invited to apply to the Publishers.

Glossary

Abbasids Arab dynasty, 750–1258 AD, with its capital at Baghdad which ruled North Africa and western Asia. In the 9th century, they frequently fought with the Byzantines, but lost effective power by the mid-10th, and eventually fell to the **Seljuks**.

Aetius Roman general who dominated the western empire for 20 years. Commander of the forces in Gaul, he almost singlehandedly preserved Roman fortunes there, defeating **Attila**, until he was treacherously murdered by the emperor in 454 AD.

Agora Marketplace, social and economic center of a Greek city, usually consisting of an open square around which most of the public buildings were constructed.

Alamanni German tribe from east of the Rhine who frequently raided Gaul and came into conflict with the Romans. In the 5th century they settled in Alsace and Switzerland, forming a kingdom which lasted until its conquest by **Clovis**.

Alans Iranian nomad people from the steppes of southern Russia, cut in two by the **Huns**. The western group joined the Germanic invasion of Gaul and eventually settled with the **Vandals** in Africa, sharing their fate. Descendants of the eastern branch still inhabit the Caucasus.

Alaric King of the **Visigoths** who had served in the Roman armies, but turned against the empire when disappointed in his hopes of high command. In 395 and 396 he ravaged Greece, then unsuccessfully invaded Italy. After the murder of **Stilicho**, he besieged Rome for plunder, set up a puppet emperor, and in 410 sacked the city. He died soon after while planning to invade Africa.

Ambrose of Milan (340–97). Governor of the region of Milan, he was proclaimed bishop of the city in 374, although he had never held church office. By his eloquence and forceful personality, he dominated the western Church, combating heresy and paganism, and successfully resisting encroachments of imperial power on the Church.

Ambulatory Covered walkway, especially inside a church behind the high altar.

Amphitheater Oval or circular building consisting of rows of seats surrounding an arena

where, in Roman times, gladiatorial combats and wild beast fights were held; in many instances, the site of Christian martyrdoms.

Anthony, Saint (c. 250–350) The first Christian monk, and founder of monasticism. At the age of 20 he withdrew from his native place to the Egyptian desert and lived in solitude and asceticism. He emerged to organize the life of the monks who had settled around him, then withdrew again to a mountain by the Red Sea where he died.

Apicius Gourmet of the time of Tiberius who reportedly committed suicide after spending most of his vast fortune on food. He was author of a cook-book which has survived in a late antique edition.

Apse Projecting part of a church, usually semicircular in plan, which contains or lies behind the main altar. In Byzantine churches, the apse almost invariably faces east.

Arcisolia Semicircular niches for receiving corpses, as found in catacombs and mausolea, frequently decorated with paintings and inscriptions.

Arcisolia

Arians Followers of Arius, a priest of Alexandria in the time of Constantine, who maintained that God the Son was created by God the Father but was of a different substance from him, a view condemned as heretical by the **Council of Nicaea**. The heresy had a wide following in the east during the 4th century and later in the west, since the Germanic tribes had been converted to Arian Christianity.

Athanasius (293–373). Bishop of Alexandria and the greatest defender of orthodoxy in the

4th century. Supported by the Egyptian Church, over which he had complete power, he faced persecution and exile for maintaining his bitter opposition to the **Arian** heresy. Many of his extensive writings have survived.

Atrium

Atrium Originally, the main open court of a Roman house. In Christian architecture, the open courtyard, surrounded by colonnades or arcades, in front of a **basilica**.

Attila King of the Huns 433–53, ruler of a dominion which stretched from the Rhine to the Caspian. After frequent threats to the eastern empire, which bought him off with huge bribes, he turned to the west, where he penetrated Gaul to be defeated near Orléans by **Aetius**. He later destroyed Aquilea, and advanced toward Rome.

Augustine (354–430). Bishop of Hippo Regius in Africa, converted to Christianity after being a pagan and a Manichaean. His vast writings are the foundation of Catholic theology; among them, the *Confessions* and the *City of God*, written to excuse the Christians for the fall of Rome in 410, are the most famous. He led the opposition to the **Donatists**, and died during the Vandal siege of Hippo.

Augustus One of the titles of the emperor, specialized in the reform of Diocletian to designate one of the two senior emperors who ruled at Nicomedia and Milan; see **Caesar**.

Austuriani Nomad tribe of the Libyan desert, swift horsemen, who supplemented their meager livelihood by robbery, and devastated the cities of Tripolitania and Cyrenaica in the 4th and 5th centuries.

Avars Turkic nomads from the Volga region who settled in the Danube basin about 560. From there they overran the Balkans with their allies the Slavs, disrupting imperial rule. In 626 they unsuccessfully besieged Constantinople in alliance with the Persians. Subsequently their power declined as the Slavs became independent, but they remained important on the Danube until they were destroyed by Charlemagne.

Bacaudae "The valiant," bands of bandits, peasants and slaves, who broke into organized revolt in Gaul in the late 3rd century. Although crushed by Maximinus in 284, their revolts and depredations were a constant menace until the end of Roman rule. During the confusion of the German invasions, in 408, they established a state in Brittany which long maintained its independence.

Bas-Empire "Low empire," name given in French to late antiquity to distinguish it from the "high empire" of the first two centuries. Sometimes extended to include the Byzantines, as in the massive history of Charles Lebeau (written 1757–86), who, like **Gibbon**, stressed the idea of decline.

Basil, Saint (c. 330–79). Bishop of Caesarea in Cappadocia and the dominant figure in the 4th-century Church. He successfully defended orthodoxy against the **Arians**, and established a rule for organizing the lives of monks which has remained fundamental in the eastern churches.

Basilica Under the Romans, a rectangular public building, usually a market or judgment hall adjacent to the **forum**. The term was adapted to Christian use to mean a long church with a nave and side aisles. There are many variations on the basic plan.

Belisarius (505–65). Roman general under Justinian, whose role in suppressing the Nika revolt earned him the command of the expedition against the **Vandals**. His swift conquest of Sicily and Africa was rewarded by a triumph and followed by his great victories in Italy. Subsequently he was replaced in Italy, but called from retirement in 559 to drive off a barbarian invasion which almost reached the capital.

Bema Chancel or sanctuary of a Greek church, the part containing the altar and the seats for the clergy.

Benedict, Saint (c. 480–544). Founder and organizer of western monasticism. Scion of a senatorial family, he fled from licentiousness and took up his abode in a cave in the mountains east of Rome. His holiness attracted many followers, and he eventually moved to Monte Casino where he founded a great monastery and imposed a rule to govern the lives of the inhabitants.

Bulgars Turkic tribe from the area between the Urals and the Volga, who crossed the Danube in 679 and set up a kingdom in territory which still bears their name. Under their first (679–1018) and second (1186–1396) empires they fiercely contested supremacy in the Balkans with the Byzantines.

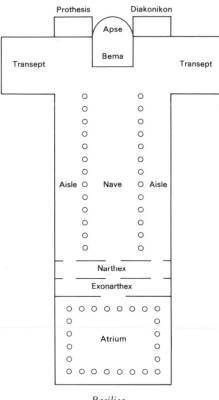

Basilica

Burgundians German tribe who crossed into Gaul in the great invasion of 406 and established themselves as allies of the Romans in eastern Gaul (Burgundy), where their kingdom was obliterated by **Attila**. A second kingdom founded in Savoy survived until the 6th century when it was taken by the **Franks**.

Bury, John Bagnell (1861–1927). English historian who, among much other work, published an important series of volumes on the period 395–867, careful and well-written studies in which he argued for a continuity between Rome and Byzantium which is now cast into doubt by the evidence of archaeology.

Caesar Under the reform of Diocletian, the title of the subordinate emperors who ruled from Sirmium, near the Danube, and Trier, near the Rhine. In theory, they were to succeed the **Augusti** on their retirement, and appoint subordinate Caesars of their own.

Caliph Literally, a "successor" (i.e. of Muhammad), title of the **Umayyad** and **Abbasid** rulers of the Arab state, later taken over by the Ottoman **sultans**.

Carausius (287–93). Commander of the fleet at Boulogne, he turned to piracy, then proclaimed himself emperor, taking over Britain, then Gaul. He defended Britain successfully until his murder, especially by a chain of strong fortresses along the **Saxon Shore**.

Catacomb Underground burial place, with numerous chambers and niches for tombs, especially favored in Italy. The Christians frequently met for pilgrimage and ritual in the catacombs of Rome.

Chosroes I King of Persia, 531–79, the greatest of the **Sasanian** dynasty. His long war with Justinian (540–62), during which his forces destroyed Antioch and overran the eastern provinces, produced no real gains, but his reform and reorganization of the government were a lasting achievement.

Chosroes II King of Persia, 589–628, launched a great war against the Romans when his benefactor, Maurice, who had restored him to the throne after a revolt, was murdered in 602. His forces saw incredible success and for a moment virtually restored the empire of the Achaemenids by conquering the region from Cilicia to Egypt. After Heraclius' successful invasion of Persia, however, he was murdered and his empire collapsed.

Chrysostom, Saint John (345–407). Priest and gifted orator of Antioch who had spent ten years in the desert, and never abandoned the ascetic ideal. As patriarch of Constantinople, 398–404, he won an enormous popular following by inveighing against the extravagance and frivolity of the day, but fell into bad repute with the government which he criticized, and died in exile.

Ciborium Canopy over the high altar in a church, usually supported by four small columns and made of stone.

Ciborium

Circus Oval or oblong space with rows of seats on three sides and a barrier down the middle, used for chariot races and other spectacles. The most famous example was the Circus Maximus in Rome.

Ciriaco D'Ancona (1391–1449). First of a long series of European travelers to the Near East to make a scientific study of antiquity. During his commercial voyages, he collected inscriptions, manuscripts, and antiquities to whose study he devoted much of his life. His works survive only in fragments.

Clovis King of the **Franks**, who began his career by defeating the last Roman resistance under **Syagrius** in 486. He later became a Christian, extended his power over the rest of Gaul, and made Paris his capital. He was the founder of the Merovingian dynasty which ruled France through the Dark Ages.

Codex Book in the modern fashion, with pages bound together, which began to replace the rolls of papyrus of antiquity in the 2nd century A D, and gained supremacy in late antiquity.

Coloni Tenant farmers who leased plots of large estates which they would work in exchange for a share of the produce. In late antiquity they became converted into serfs, with no freedom of movement. The state ultimately depended on them for its revenues.

Conch Semicircular niche crowned by a half-dome, frequently used for shrines within churches.

Count of Africa Under the reforms of Diocletian, commander of the Roman army in the diocese of Africa, which included modern Algeria, Tunisia and western Libya.

Covel, John (1638–1722). Master of Christ's College, Cambridge, who, as chaplain to the Levant Company, spent 1670–77 in Turkey. He wrote several works on his travels, being especially interested in the Greek Church for material which English bishops sought in their disputes with Rome.

Cross-in-Square Church Church plan in which the center of the building forms a cross which supports the dome and is in turn inscribed within a square chamber.

Cumans Turkic tribe who settled in the region of the Dniepr in the mid-11th century. From there, they frequently attacked the Russians, Bulgarians and Byzantines, who were obliged to fight several wars against them. Their state was finally destroyed by the Mongols in 1239.

Curzon, Robert (1810–73). Traveled in Egypt, Palestine, Greece and Albania, visiting monasteries in the hope of finding unknown manuscripts. His *Visit to the Monasteries of the Levant*, published in 1849 and written with great charm, was of considerable scientific importance.

Cyril and Methodius Two brothers from Thessalonica who carried on missionary work in Bohemia and Moravia, 863–85, known as the "Apostles to the Slavs." By creating an alphabet for the Slavic language which is still used and by preaching in Slavic they enabled Byzantine Christianity to gain firm root in the Balkans, although the area where they preached soon returned to western Catholicism.

Dark Ages In Byzantine history, the term often applied to the period of the invasions – from the 7th to the mid-9th century, so called because the sources are poor and little is known.

De Officiis Manual of Byzantine court ceremonial compiled under John Kantakouzenos. Its descriptions of court ritual and its lists of office-holders according to their rank make it a valuable source for administrative history.

Decurion Member of a council which ruled the municipalities into which the empire was divided, charged with collecting the local taxes. Under the empire, many served voluntarily, but in late antiquity compulsion was introduced as the demands of the state increased. The decurions, renowned for their rapacity and zeal to escape into higher office, were a valuable and fundamental part of the machinery of government until Justinian.

Deesis

Deesis Scene, frequent in church mosaics, showing the Virgin Mary and John the Baptist interceding with Christ for the sins of the world.

Diakonikon Room attached to a church, usually adjacent to the apse, used as vestry, archive and for storage of offerings.

Diehl, Charles (1859–1944). One of the most important modern scholars in Byzantine studies, whose works on Ravenna, Byzantine Africa and Justinian are of lasting value. He also wrote many popular works which stimulated considerable interest in Byzantium.

Digenes Akritas Byzantine epic, probably composed in the mid-11th century. It narrates the adventures of the hero after whom it is named: a border warrior of mixed Christian and Muslim parentage who fought valiantly against the Arabs on the eastern frontier.

Donatists Heretical Christian sect of North Africa, which broke from the Church over the question of admitting back into communion those who had handed over the scriptures during the Great Persecution. Although declared heretic by Constantine and persecuted for a century, the sect had numerous adherents, often fanatical, and great influence in Africa.

Du Cange, Charles du Fresne, Sieur (1610–88). Founder of modern Byzantine studies, holder of a government sinecure which enabled him to spend 20 years of research in the archives of Paris. Among his extensive writings are dictionaries of medieval Greek and Latin, and works on the Latin empire, Constantinople and Byzantine genealogy, all still fundamental.

Dualism System of belief which recognizes the two opposing forces of Good and Evil as supreme in the world. Such doctrines were fundamental for Zoroastrianism, Mithraism and the semi-Christian Manichaeans, and had great influence on the **Paulicians**.

Duces Under the reform of Diocletian, commanders of the provincial armies, most of them on the frontier. Each controlled an area usually equal to a civil province. Duces were chosen from regimental commanders, and rarely rose to high positions.

Embolos Term used in late antiquity to designate a street lined with colonnades, behind which were usually shops or houses.

Emir "Commander," title given to the Arab **caliphs**, to generals and to the rulers of the Turkish principalities in Asia Minor.

Ephesus, Council of (449). Known as the "Robber Council," dominated by the bishop of Alexandria and the **Monophysites**, who beat down all opposition to proclaim their doctrine orthodox. Its decrees were annulled, and it is not recognized as an ecumenical council.

Eusebius (c. 260–c. 340). Bishop of Caesarea in Palestine and, as ecclesiastical advisor to the

Emperor Constantine, one of the most influential churchmen of his age. Among his many writings, his *History of the Church* and *Life of Constantine* have survived to be fundamental sources for the Church and the age.

Exarch Title of the governors of Italy and Africa, who had both civil and military powers. The governments were set up by Maurice to secure the severely threatened provinces and are thought to have been models for the **theme** system.

Faction Organizers and supporters of the teams which raced in the **Hippodrome**, named for the racing colors, Blues and Greens. In most cities, the population was divided between the two factions whose violent quarrels were a constant source of sedition until the reign of Justinian.

Fallmerayer, Jakob Philipp (1790–1861). German historian, author of the *History of the Empire of Trebizond* (1827) and *History of the Peloponnesus in the Middle Ages* (1830–36), best known for his unwelcome (and exaggerated) view that the Greeks of his day were of Slavic or Albanian descent without a drop of true Greek blood.

Filioque Doctrinal difference between the eastern and western Churches. The Catholics believed that the Holy Spirit proceeded from the father *and the son* (*filioque*) and added that to the Creed. The Orthodox rejected the innovation, and used it as the basis for their schism under **Photios**. It remained an irreconcilable point of dispute between the two churches.

Finlay, George (1799–1875). English historian whose participation in the Greek revolution led him to write the history of Greece from the Roman conquest until his own time, a work of great influence which drew the attention of the English-speaking world to the post-Classical period.

Florence, Council of Church council held under Pope Eugenius IV in 1439, attended by the emperor John VIII, the patriarch of Constantinople and other Orthodox dignitaries, who signed an act of union with the western Church, in the hope of western aid against the Turks. Like the Council of **Lyons**, it resolved nothing, since the Byzantine populace was hostile to the idea of union.

Forum Marketplace and center of public business in a Roman city. In Roman colonies, it usually occupied the center of the site and contained temples as well as a judgment-hall and shops. The term came to mean merely an open square.

Franks Group of Germanic tribes established on the northern part of the Rhine frontier who carried out serious attacks on Gaul in the 4th and 5th centuries. As the Romans withdrew from the Rhine, the Franks moved into northern Gaul and eventually, under **Clovis**, came to rule the whole province, which takes its modern name, France, from them.

Galla Placidia (388–450). Daughter of Theodosius and sister of Honorius, she was taken captive by Alaric during the sack of Rome, remained with the Goths five years, and married their king Ataulf. After his death, she was returned to Rome in exchange for 600,000 measures of grain, and married the general Constantius, long her suitor. Regent for her ineffectual son Valentinian III, 423–36. Her mausoleum in Ravenna is one of the outstanding monuments of the age.

Garum Sauce made of fish pickled in brine for 2 or 3 months, used universally in Roman cooking in place of salt and as a flavoring.

Gibbon, Edward (1737–94). English historian who, while "musing amidst the ruins of the Capitol" in 1764, was inspired to write the *History of the Decline and Fall of The Roman Empire*, a literary masterpiece completed in 1787, which has never been surpassed in style, judgment or comprehensive research.

Gildo Moorish chief who rose to be **Count of Africa** under Theodosius, on whose death he broke into rebellion and cut off the grain supply of Rome. The revolt was suppressed in 398, Gildo was executed, and his vast estates confiscated.

Goths Germanic tribe originally inhabiting the Baltic region, who extended their domains to the Danube and the Black Sea in the 3rd century, and from there invaded the Balkans and Asia Minor, inflicting severe defeats on the Romans. Later they broke up into the **Ostrogoths** and **Visigoths**.

Governors Heads of civil administration in the provinces, subordinate to the **vicars** and **praetorian prefects**. The office was usually held for a short time, and was a valuable stage in an official career. Their power grew as the municipalities declined, but the office vanished with the militarization of the administration in the 7th century.

Gregory the Great Descendant of a rich senatorial family, he founded monasteries in Sicily and Italy and became a monk. As pope, 590–604, he reorganized and strengthened the Church by sending out missions and by enforcing papal authority in civil as well as ecclesiastical matters. He clearly established the supremacy of the pope in the west and exercised virtually imperial power in Italy.

Guiscard, Robert Leader of the Normans in Italy, who successfully drove the Byzantines from Italy by conquering Bari in 1071, then embarked on the conquest of Sicily. In 1081 he crossed over to the Balkans, defeated Alexios Komnenos and took Durazzo, aiming to conquer the empire. He died of disease after being defeated by the Byzantines and Venetians in 1085.

Helen (c. 247–327). Wife of Constantius I and mother of Constantine. Late in life she reputedly made a pilgrimage to Jerusalem, where she discovered the **True Cross**. She is recognized as a saint by the Greek Church and is generally represented with her son, also a saint.

Heruli Germanic tribe who joined the **Goths** during the reign of Gallienus in devastating Asia Minor; their invasion of Greece in 267 was especially destructive. Later, they fought with Romans or barbarians and disappear from history in the 6th century.

Hippodrome Racecourse, especially for the chariot races favored in late antiquity; essentially

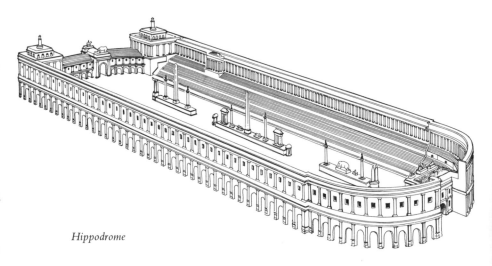

Hippodrome

a long, enclosed grandstand rounded at both ends. The most famous was at Constantinople, where the emperor would appear before the populace who could there express their views.

Hopf, Karl (1832–73). German professor who devoted his life to the study of Greece under Frankish rule (after 1204). He did extensive research in Greece and in European archives, and compiled a work which is invaluable for the amount of inaccessible material it incorporates.

Huns Nomadic tribe of central Asia who moved into Europe in the 4th century. They crushed the **Goths**, then settled in the Danube basin for 50 years, from which they ravaged the Roman empire. After the death of their chief **Attila**, their power soon faded.

Icon Image of Christ, the Virgin, or a saint, in painting or mosaic. Interiors of churches were usually covered with icons, but the term is frequently used to refer to small portable paintings on wooden tablets. Icons were (and are) greatly favored by the Orthodox Church.

Iconoclast "Breaker of images." Name applied to a reforming party in Byzantium which wanted to eliminate **icons** and the superstitions which went with them. The iconoclasts came to power under Leo III in the mid-8th century and remained prominent until the Council of 843. As a result of their work, little is known of earlier Byzantine painting, and sculpture in the round was abandoned.

Isaurians Tribe of the mountains of southern Asia Minor, famous for their banditry. They rose in revolt several times in the 3rd and 4th centuries, then became so important in the Roman army that one of their chiefs became emperor under the name Zeno. After his death, they again revolted, but were definitively suppressed by Anastasius.

Krum King of Bulgaria, c. 800–14. Under his dominion, the **Bulgars** gained in strength, capturing Serdica (Sofia) in 809, destroying the Byzantine army and killing the emperor in 811. In 1813 Krum laid siege to Constantinople unsuccessfully, vowing to return, but he died the next year.

Krumbacher, Karl (1856–1909). Founder of Byzantine studies in Germany, and of the major periodical in the field. His comprehensive *History of Byzantine Literature* is still an indispensable work of reference.

Leake, Colonel William (1777–1860). English topographer and antiquarian who served in Turkey, Greece and Egypt in the early 19th century. The fruit of his researches is contained in several valuable works on topography and numismatics, of which *Travels in the Morea* (1830) and *Travels in Northern Greece* (1835) are the best known.

Mehmet II

Lombards Germanic tribe who left the Danube region after the arrival of the **Avars** and descended on Italy in 568. They quickly conquered the north and center, dividing the peninsula with the Byzantines, whose supremacy they did not recognize. They conquered Ravenna in 751, but in 774 were defeated by Charlemagne and ceased to exist as a kingdom.

Lyons, Second Council of Synod called by Pope Gregory X in 1274 to reform clerical morals and make arrangements for a new crusade. During it, the Byzantine legates accepted reunion with the western Church, an act which roused bitter hostility in the empire.

Magyars Nomad people of the southern Russian steppe, called in by the Byzantines to attack **Symeon** of Bulgaria. They were driven westward by the **Pechenegs** in 896 and settled in the Danube basin, from which they inflicted devastating raids on Europe. After the coronation of their king, Saint Stephen, in 1001, they became Christian and settled, as the Hungarian kingdom. The Hungarians are their descendants.

Martin of Tours (316–400). Christian, who after serving in the Roman army, devoted himself to asceticism and became one of the founders of monasticism in the west. He opposed the **Arians** and, as bishop of Tours (371–400), did much to destroy paganism in Gaul.

Martyrium Structure built on a site associated with the memory of a martyr, varying from a simple apse or courtyard protecting the martyr's grave to an elaborate precinct. May also indicate a church built in honor of a martyr.

Maximus of Ephesus Most famous pagan philosopher and miracle worker of the 4th century. Julian fell under his influence while a

student at Pergamum, and invited him to the capital when he became emperor. Maximus had tremendous influence during Julian's reign, but was executed in 371 in the persecution of magicians carried out by Valens.

Mehmet II Ottoman sultan, 1421–51, a man of learning and taste, famous for his conquest of Constantinople in 1453. He also expanded his empire in Europe and Asia and even, just before his death, established a foothold in Italy.

Metropolitan Bishop of a provincial capital. Because the organization of the Church was modeled on that of the state, he had jurisdiction over the bishops of the province whose boundaries remained the same regardless of civil changes. The metropolitans ruled the Church along with the **patriarch**.

Milvian Bridge Bridge over the Tiber, immediately north of Rome, where Constantine saw his vision of the Cross and defeated Maxentius in 312.

Mithra Persian god of the sun, whose worship spread to the Roman Empire in the 1st century AD. As the Unconquered Sun, the favorite god of the army, Mithra's cult spread to every part of the empire, was the focus for state religion under Aurelian, and was dominant until Constantine, gradually yielding to Christianity in the 4th century.

Monconys, Balthasar (1611–65). French traveler, whose predilection for the occult led him to seek the traces of Zoroastrianism in the east. He visited the Near East and Turkey in 1645–49.

Monophysites Adherents of a Christian faction which believed that Christ had a single nature instead of two (human and divine). The heresy originated in Egypt in the mid-5th century and soon commanded the fierce adherence of the eastern provinces. The opposition of these regions to the theology of Constantinople is supposed to have facilitated the Arab conquests.

Moors Berber-speaking tribes of the mountains of North Africa, who long contested rule of the region with Romans and Byzantines. By the end of the 3rd century, they had taken over the western provinces; later, they rendered the Byzantine reconquest precarious. Many Moors, like **Gildo**, rose high in imperial service.

Mosaic Form of decoration in which the design is formed of small colored cubes; the Byzantines particularly favored colored glass. Under the Romans, mosaics were most commonly used for floors, but they mounted to walls and ceilings by late antiquity and remained the preferred form of church decoration for the Byzantines.

Mottraye, Aubry de la (1674–1743). Originally a Protestant minister, he spent a large part of his life traveling in the Ottoman empire and Europe. The narrative of his journeys, which contains much curious information, was published in both English and French.

Narthex Vestibule of a church, which precedes the nave and aisles and is separated from them by a wall or row of columns. In the early church the place from which candidates for baptism and penitents could observe the service.

Nicaea, Council of First ecumenical council, held in 325 to condemn the doctrines of the **Arians**. Constantine presided over the Council, thus establishing the supremacy of the emperor in the eastern Church.

Nicaea, Second Council of Seventh ecumenical council, held under Irene in 787, and attended by 350 bishops and many monks. It reversed the iconoclastic council of 754 and restored reverence for the images. It is the last council to be recognized as ecumenical by the Orthodox Church.

Mosaic

Odaenathus Ruler of the caravan city of Palmyra in the Syrian desert. After the defeat and capture of Valerian in 260, he defended the Roman cause in the east, suppressing usurpers and inflicting severe defeats on the Persians. Assassinated in 267.

Odo of Deuil French monk who accompanied King Louis VII on the Second Crusade (1147–48). His letters home, combined into a single narrative, are the main source for the crusade in Asia Minor, and full of invective against the Byzantines.

Odoacer (or Odovacar). Germanic general who gained supreme power in Italy with the help of the barbarian troops there in 476, and deposed the last western emperor, Romulus Augustulus. He ruled Italy as the nominal vassal of the eastern emperor, but when he became too powerful, the emperor sent against him Theodoric the **Ostrogoth**, by whom he was defeated and killed in 493.

Osman Traditional founder and first ruler (1290–1326) of the **Ottoman** dynasty. He converted his nomad tribe of the Byzantine

frontier into a settled state with at least one large city under its control.

Ostrogoths "East Goths," conquered by **Attila**. On the breakup of the Hunnic empire, they moved into the Balkans. Their king Theodoric (471–526) gained high Roman positions, and led his people into Italy where they established a kingdom. After their defeat by Justinian, the Ostrogoths recrossed the Alps and vanished from history.

Ottomans Turkish tribe named for their first historical ruler, **Osman** (1290–1326). Settled by the **Seljuks** as border guards in Bithynia on the Byzantine frontier, they expanded at the expense of the empire, soon taking the cities of Bithynia, and in 1354 crossing into Europe, where they rapidly conquered the Balkans. The dynasty founded by Osman ruled Turkey until 1922.

Pachomius, Saint (292–346). Egyptian monk, organizer of Christian monastic life. After serving in the army, he became a Christian in 314, and withdrew to the desert to become a hermit. He devoted much of his life to organizing monasteries and a common life for the great crowds of monks in Egypt, work which had a permanent influence.

Paparregopoulos, K. Modern Greek historian whose five-volume *History of the Greek People from the Most Ancient Times to Recent Years* appeared in Athens in 1860–77. The work is important for the attention which it devotes to the Byzantine period and notorious for its biased and nationalistic viewpoint.

Patriarch Honorary title designating archbishops whose authority extended over large areas. In late antiquity the bishops of Constantinople, Antioch, Jerusalem and Alexandria held the title, but in the Byzantine period it generally refers to the head of the Church in Constantinople.

Paulicians Christian sect who rejected images and the Cross, allegorized much Christian doctrine, and incorporated many elements of **dualism**. They were strong in eastern Asia Minor and, after a violent persecution under Theodora, established an independent state at Tephrice beyond the eastern frontier whence they attacked the empire until crushed by Basil I. Many were transplanted to Bulgaria, where they spread their doctrine.

Pechenegs (or Patzinaks) Turkic tribe from the steppes of southern Russia. Driven from their homeland in 889, they were called in by **Symeon** of Bulgaria to attack the **Magyars**, whose lands between the Danube and the Don they occupied. They were of considerable importance in Byzantine diplomacy as a possible counterweight to the Bulgarians, Russians or Magyars, but they frequently attacked the

empire, even besieging Constantinople in 1090, until they were defeated and dispersed in 1122.

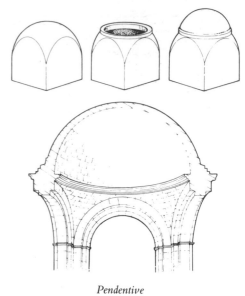

Pendentive

Pendentive Wall made of a segment of a sphere used to support a dome on arches of columns.

Peristyle Courtyard surrounded by colonnades, frequent in late antique houses and public buildings.

Phanariots Name applied to the Greek families who provided the princes of Wallachia and Moldavia (modern Romania) under the Ottomans, 1711–1821, so called from the Phanar quarter of Istanbul.

Photios (c. 820–91). Imperial secretary who rose to become patriarch of Constantinople, 858–67 and 878–86. He opposed what he felt were the pretensions of the pope to supremacy and provoked the first major schism between the eastern and western Churches. He strengthened the Church and encouraged much missionary activity. He was of great learning, and a patron of education; many of his works survive.

Postumus (259–68). General of the army of the Rhine under Valerian. He revolted and set up an independent state, ruling Gaul, Britain and Spain from his capital at Trier. He successfully defended his domains against the emperor and the barbarians until he was killed by his own troops for refusing to allow them to sack the city of Mainz, which had rebelled.

Pouqueville, François (1770–1838). French traveler who accompanied the campaign of Napoleon to Egypt and on his return was captured by Barbary corsairs and imprisoned in Greece and Istanbul for three years. From this developed a lifelong interest in the Levant, reinforced by subsequent voyages, which produced numerous valuable accounts of the region.

Praetorian Prefect Originally the head of the emperor's bodyguard, the prefect evolved to become chief of the civil government under Diocletian. There were four prefects, each responsible for the administration of a vast area; the prefect of the east, who controlled Thrace, the Near East and Egypt, was the most powerful officer after the emperor. The office disappeared in the Dark Ages.

Prothesis Room attached to a church, usually adjacent to the **apse**, used for the preparation and storage of the materials for Holy Communion.

Ramsay, Sir William Mitchell (1851–1939). Classical scholar and archaeologist who carried out continuous explorations in Asia Minor, 1880–1914. As professor at Aberdeen, he founded an important school which has carried on his researches. He wrote several books and innumerable articles on Asia Minor and the early history of the Church. His *Historical Geography of Asia Minor* (1890), though replete with errors of fact and method, has not been replaced.

Rotunda Round building, especially one covered with a dome, a form sometimes used in late antiquity for mausolea and churches.

Rotunda

Sandys, George (1578–1644). Observant English traveler who visited Turkey, Egypt and the Holy Land in 1610–11. He published the account of his voyage, but is best known for his role in the Virginia Colony, and his translation of Ovid's *Metamorphoses*.

Sasanians Powerful, nationalistic dynasty who ruled Persia from 226 to 651, frequently contesting rule of the Near East with the Romans. The government was highly centralized and strongly Zoroastrian.

Saxon Shore East and southeast coast of England, so called because it was exposed to

attacks by the Saxons and other tribes from Germany. It was defended by a series of powerful fortresses begun under Carausius and strengthened by his successors through the 4th century.

Schism Break in relations between the eastern and western Churches, especially the great schism of 1054, after which Orthodox and Catholics were no longer in communion. This had been foreshadowed by the so-called "Photian schism" of the late 10th century.

Scriptorium

Schlumberger, Gustave (1844–1928). French historian and popularizer of Byzantine studies, who did important work in the study of coins and seals. His monumentally verbose works on the 10th and 11th centuries, though little read today, were extremely popular and have never been replaced.

Scriptorium Room or building in a monastery set aside for writing and copying of manuscripts, a fundamental role of the monasteries which made them centers of learning and preservers of the Classical heritage.

Seljuks Turkish tribe from Central Asia who conquered Persia in the early 11th century, took Baghdad in 1055, where their leader was proclaimed sultan, and shortly after began attacking Byzantine Asia Minor. After their great victory at Manzikert in 1071, they established a state in Asia Minor, with its capital at Konya (Iconium), which lasted until the late 13th century.

Senate Originally a council with a major role in affairs of state, but reduced in late antiquity to a

body of rich and influential men. Membership of the two senates at Rome and Constantinople was a valued and highly coveted privilege. The senate continued to exist through the Byzantine period in a ceremonial role.

Seven Churches of Asia Christian communities of Asia Minor which St John the Divine addressed in the Book of Revelation, namely Ephesus, Smyrna, Pergamum, Thyateira, Sardis, Philadelphia and Laodicea.

Slavs Group of peoples speaking an Indo-European language, originally from central eastern Europe. They gradually expanded to the west and south and in the 6th and 7th centuries poured into the Balkans under the domination of the **Avars**. Except for Greece, colonized by the Byzantines, their settlements in the peninsula have been permanent.

Spina Barrier along the center of the **hippodrome** around which the chariots raced; sometimes decorated, as at Constantinople, with statues and other works of art.

Spoils Pieces of older structures, statues, inscriptions etc., reused as building material in new constructions.

Spon, Jacob (1647–85). Physician and antiquarian of Lyons, who made a long journey to Greece and Turkey in 1674–76, during which he collected over 200 inscriptions and much valuable information which he published in detail. He wrote many other works on antiquity and medicine.

Squinch Series of small arches placed across the corners of a square chamber to convert its upper part into an octagon, on which a dome can be superimposed.

Squinch

Stilicho Vandal who commanded Roman armies under Theodosius, and was made guardian of the young emperor Honorius, who married his daughter. He successfully defended Italy against all attacks until his murder in 408.

Strategos In the militarized administrative system of the **themes**, the governor of a district.

The word retained its original meaning of "general."

Strzygowski, Josef (1862–1941). Austrian art critic and historian who first appreciated the importance of Asia Minor in the history of Christian art and architecture and published several pioneering and influential works on the subject.

Stylite

Stylite Ascetic who showed his holiness by living on top of a pillar, a fashion begun and made famous by St Simeon of Antioch (389–459), and followed by many in late antiquity, with a revival in the 10th and 11th centuries.

Stylobate Continuous stone foundation on which the columns or piers of a building rest.

Sueves Name of a group of Germanic tribes. One crossed the Rhine in 406 and devastated Gaul before founding a kingdom in northwest Spain which survived until it was conquered by the **Visigoths** in the 6th century. Another branch of the same people settled in southwest Germany where they have given their name to Swabia.

Sultan Title given to the ruler of the Ottoman empire. It was first officially applied to the Seljuk rulers of Mesopotamia in the 11th century to indicate that they exercised material power on behalf of the **caliph**.

Syagrius Last defender of Roman Gaul, who controlled the northern part of the province from 464 to 486 after the rest had fallen to the Germans. He was defeated by **Clovis** at Soissons and subsequently executed.

Symeon Tsar of Bulgaria, 893–927. Educated at Constantinople and deeply impressed with Byzantine culture, he encouraged its growth in Bulgaria where he established a new and splendid capital. Although obliged to spend much of his reign fighting the **Magyars**, he had pretentions to be emperor and inflicted severe defeats on the Byzantines, twice besieging Constantinople.

Tetrapylon Four-sided monumental arch, commonly built at the intersection of two major streets, and often marking the center of a late antique city or quarter.

Tetrarchy "Rule of a fourth," a term applied in modern times to the government of Diocletian with its four emperors – two **Augusti** and two **Caesars**.

Texier, Charles (1802–71). French archaeologist who made extensive scientific voyages in Asia Minor in 1833–37 and 1839. The results are published in the three monumental folios of his *Description de l'Asie mineure* (1838–48), a work full of detailed plans, drawings and observations.

Theme Province in the militarized Byzantine administration of the 7th century and later, named from a word which also meant "army." In this system, the army originally had control of a province, which was governed by a **strategos**, or general.

Thomas the Slav Byzantine general, companion in arms of Michael of Amorium and Leo V. When the latter was murdered, Thomas led a revolt which gained the adherence of most of Asia Minor. He proclaimed himself the champion of the icons, and besieged Constantinople, where he was defeated in 823. His rebellion so weakened the empire that the Arabs were able shortly after to seize Crete and descend on Sicily.

Timur (or Tamerlane) Mongol ruler (1369–1405), famous for his fabulous conquests, which stretched from the frontiers of China to Asia Minor, where his whirlwind campaign temporarily broke the power of the Ottomans. His empire disintegrated on his death.

Transept Part of a church perpendicular to the nave, between it and the apse; in a **basilica** it gives the building a somewhat cruciform plan.

True Cross Cross on which Christ was executed. It was later buried and miraculously discovered by **Helen** in 326. A church was built to receive the relic, and another in Rome (S. Croce in Gerusalemme) for a piece sent there. Removed from Jerusalem by **Chosroes II**, it was restored by Heraclius, then brought to Constantinople during the Arab conquests.

Tsar Russian and Bulgarian title of king, derived ultimately from Caesar. Similarly, in those languages Constantinople is called Tsarigrad, "the city of the tsar."

Umayyads Arab dynasty with their capital at Damascus who ruled (661–750) a vast area eventually stretching from Spain to Central Asia, and frequently came into conflict with the Byzantines. Umayyad caliphs sent out the two great expeditions against Constantinople in 673 and 716.

Vandals Germanic tribe originally from south Germany, who moved to the Danube in the 3rd century, and in 406 crossed the Rhine to devastate France before settling in Spain. In 429 the whole nation crossed into Africa, which they soon conquered, establishing a kingdom which lasted until their defeat by Justinian; thereafter, they vanish from history.

Vicar Under the system of Diocletian, an official of the **praetorian prefect** who had fiscal and judicial authority over several provinces grouped in a diocese. By the time of Justinian, the office was felt to be unnecessary and generally abolished.

Visigoths One of the nations of the **Goths**, who crossed the Roman frontier in 376, fleeing the invasion of **Attila**. Settled in the Balkans after the battle of Adrianople, they soon moved on to Italy, sacking Rome in 410, before establishing a kingdom in southern Gaul (419–507) and then in Spain (507–711).

Wood, John Turtle (1820–90). English architect and archaeologist, the first to carry out scientific excavation in Asia Minor. He dug at Ephesus from 1863 to 1874 and succeeded by 1869 in his primary aim of discovering the deeply buried remains of the temple of Artemis, once one of the wonders of the ancient world.

Zenobia Widow of **Odaenathus**, she took control of Palmyra on her husband's assassination and established an independent state which at its peak controlled Egypt, Syria and half of Asia Minor. She was finally defeated by Aurelian in 272, adorned his triumph, and retired to a villa near Rome.

Index